PHILOSOPHY AS A SCIENCE

PHILOSOPHY AS A SCIENCE

ITS MATTER AND ITS METHOD

By

C. J. DUCASSE

PROFESSOR OF PHILOSOPHY
BROWN UNIVERSITY

20975

NEW YORK
OSKAR PIEST
1941

Preface

AMONG the tasks of philosophy there is one that has no analogue among those of any of the other branches of knowledge. Consider, for instance, chemistry and its relation to problems such as what the distinctive subject matter of chemistry is, what chemists seek to know about it, how it and the investigation of it are related to other sorts of human endeavor, what sort of value chemistry has for human beings, etc. Such problems are perhaps discussed by a chemist when he is called upon to give a public address or to set the stage for his introductory course at the beginning of his first lecture; but they are not problems of chemistry itself. They belong rather to the philosophy of chemistry, and persons other than chemists may easily be more competent to deal with them than chemists would be.

The situation is the same in the other sciences, but in philosophy it is radically different. What subject matter is peculiar to philosophy, what questions about it are philosophical, what method is appropriate to the solving of them, how philosophizing is related to what chemists, mathematicians, poets, stockbrokers, manufacturers, etc., do, what philosophy contributes to the life of man—all these are genuinely philosophical questions. They belong to a branch of inquiry which, although seldom explicitly included in lists of the philosophical disciplines, is unquestionably one of them. This discipline is the philosophy of philosophy. In other fields of knowledge nothing parallel to it is to be found: there is no such thing as, for instance, the chemistry of chemistry or the botany of botany.

It is to this branch of philosophy that the present work belongs. It represents an attempt to formulate an answer more specific, more detailed, and more defensible than the common ones to the question the layman so often asks of the philosopher, viz., What *is* philosophy? Seldom, I fear, does the philosopher reply to it in a manner really satisfactory to his inquirer or even, I venture to say, to himself. It has plagued me for twenty years or more, and many are the attempts I have made to find for it an answer both clear-cut and of the truth of which I could feel confident. It seems to me now at last that I have succeeded, but of this the reader is to be the judge.

The principal contentions argued in this book, which together define my answer, are that knowledge, in the same sense which the term has for the natural and other sciences, is what philosophy seeks; that philosophy therefore attempts to be genuinely a science, and that its method must accordingly be as scientific—as truly knowledge-yielding—as that of any other science, while its subject matter is distinct from that of any of the other sciences; that in philosophy as in the other sciences we have to distinguish between "primitive" and "derivative" subject matter, and that the primitive subject matter of philosophy is appraisals—ethical, logical, epistemic, ontological, aesthetic, and other; that appraisals are always ultimately relative to persons; that in philosophy, as in any other science, observation of particular facts, empirical generalization of them, and theoretical explanation, systematization, correction, and supplementation of the empirical generalizations all are intrinsic parts of the knowledge-seeking task; that norms are generalized appraisals; that wisdom is knowledge of norms; that knowledge of norms may be either only empirical and correspondingly limited and precarious, or in addition theoretically systematized, supplemented, and corrected, and correspondingly comprehensive and firm; and that philosophy is the methodical search for wisdom, while the application of wisdom to the concrete problems of life is not philosophy but philosophical engineering.

The bare recital of these contentions is enough to indicate that the theory of the nature of philosophy which they outline differs sharply from both of the accounts of philosophy that are perhaps most in the public eye today, viz., John Dewey's and Rudolph Carnap's. The various statements to be found in Dewey's writings as to what philosophy is or should be are not easy or perhaps even possible to integrate into one unambiguous and consistent account. But they seem to me in any case on the whole to describe not philosophy itself but philosophical engineering, and indeed chiefly or only the branch of philosophical engineering that concerns itself with concrete problems of the ethical and social kinds.

The other account of philosophy attracting attention today is that of which Carnap has been the chief exponent. According to him, philosophy is the logical syntax of the language of science; and those of the traditional problems of metaphysics, epistemology, ethics, etc., which are not syntactical are only pseudo-problems. Although I believe not only that Carnap does not prove these contentions but also that they are erroneous, I agree that *some* of the traditional problems of philosophy are pseudo-problems. Accordingly, I believe that the attack of the logical positivists upon traditional philosophy has been salutary, for their demand for strictness of statement and for the credentials of the assertions one makes is tending to discourage the logically loose and empirically irresponsible sort of "philosophizing" which has only too often brought into disrepute the name of philosophy.

Some of the material in this volume has already appeared, although mostly in somewhat different shape, as articles in philosophical journals. This is true of chapters iii, vii, xi, and xii, and of short passages in some other chapters. For permission to make use of the contents of these articles thanks are due, respectively, to the editors of the *Journal of Philosophy*, to the University of Chicago Press and the editors of *Ethics*, and to the editors of the *Philosophical Review*. To my colleagues, Drs. W. C. Barrett and M. H. Hepp and Professors C. A. Baylis and R. M. Blake, I am under great obligation for valuable comments either on the manuscript itself or on some of the ideas contained in it, which they have heard me express at various times. I am conscious of a similar obligation also to the succession of able graduate students whom I have been privileged to teach over a number of years. One of them, Mr. Vincent Tomas, I have to thank also for the preparation of the index.

C. J. DUCASSE

PROVIDENCE, R. I.
MARCH 14, 1941

TABLE OF CONTENTS

PART I

SOME RECENT HYPOTHESES AS TO THE NATURE AND METHOD OF PHILOSOPHY

Introduction

PHILOSOPHY, like the sciences, has been pursuing its inquiries for hundreds of years. The sciences, by this time, have succeeded in winning a vast body of knowledge, and daily make positive additions to it, notwithstanding their theoretical controversies. In philosophy, on the other hand, a very different picture presents itself. What we find there is rather

> that all new theories do but add to the babel and confusion, that there is no cumulative co-operative advance from generation to generation, no funded stock of philosophical truths which can be taught as its established rudiments to beginners, and which are taken for granted by all experts as the basis of further enquiry. The same problems are ever examined afresh . . . the old problems remain persistently open.[1]

The difference between the case of philosophy and that of natural science is described by another writer as follows:

> Science shows a gradual development. . . . . It cannot be seriously doubted for an instant that we know very much more about nature, for example, than people living in former centuries knew. There is unquestionably some kind of advance shown in science, but if we are perfectly honest, a similar kind of advance cannot be discovered in philosophy. The same great issues are discussed nowadays that were discussed in the time of Plato. When for a time it seemed as though a certain question were definitely settled, soon the same question comes up again and has to be discussed and reconsidered.[2]

In this state of affairs, one is moved to wonder whether philosophy is doomed to remain forever not only inconclu-

---

[1] This indictment of philosophy is from R. F. A. Hoernlé's *Studies in Contemporary Metaphysics* (p. 48). His own attitude in this connection seems to be that, although the allegations are true, they are more or less irrelevant, because philosophy attempts something fundamentally different from what science aims at.

[2] Moritz Schlick, *The Future of Philosophy*, College of the Pacific Publications in Philosophy, I (1932), p. 48.

sive, but inconclusive always concerning the same problems; or whether, on the contrary, knowledge and positive progress are possible in its field in the same sense as in the sciences.

This question leads one in turn to ask why the success of philosophy in solving its problems has been so much less than that of science in respect to its particular sphere. The ultimate answer is perhaps that the task of philosophy is more elusive and more difficult than that of natural science. Such a suspicion is confirmed by the fact that when a scientist, rendered confident by his successes in science, turns his attention to some of the problems of philosophy, the result of his attempts to solve them is in most cases even less felicitous than that achieved by philosophers.[3]

But no real task, of course, is intrinsically difficult. The difficulty a task presents is a matter only of the equipment at our disposal. In the case of tasks of inquiry, equipment means chiefly a clear realization of the nature of the problem to be solved on the one hand, and, on the other, knowledge of the sort of method appropriate to the solution of problems of the nature given. Lack of this equipment is probably the chief reason why the philosopher's search for knowledge has met with relatively so little success. Philosophical writings—often even those of philosophers considered great—are notable for their use of highly ambiguous terms, their extreme vagueness of statement, their acceptance of hypotheses without adequate verification, and for transitions of thought logically too irresponsible to deserve the name of inference. It may well be that fruits—of certain sorts—may be obtained

---

[3] See for example P. W. Bridgman's recent volume, *The Nature of Physical Theory.* The merits of Bridgman's essential contention are obscured instead of demonstrated by the numerous confusions and the indefensible assertions to which these lead, and with which the first five chapters especially abound.

notwithstanding, or even by means of, such procedures. But those fruits cannot be of the sort called knowledge.

In any novel task the first steps are the hardest and the slowest. The task of winning knowledge is no exception to this rule, for before it can proceed apace, its preliminary effort must discover, by the slow process of trial and error, both what kinds of problems are illusory and what are the genuine problems capable of solution. It must also discover methods adapted to the inquiry. Thus, a long period of groping and methodological blundering is unavoidable before the significant problems of any field of inquiry, the nature of knowledge-yielding method in general, or the particular manner of applying that method to a given field, becomes fully clear. During that period, progress necessarily consists in the exploration of blind alleys for the most part, and at this stage the exploration of them is itself unsystematic. Progress of this kind is not obvious even to those who make it and, as in the exploration of a dark labyrinth, the task may easily seem the more hopeless the longer one labors at it. But with persistence an alley which is not blind is here and there found, and with even the dim light it provides, further search becomes a little easier. Of success in the search for knowledge it is certainly true that to them that have some, more shall be given.

The emergence of the physical sciences from their period of groping is a recent affair, and as a result of it these sciences have made more progress in the last hundred years than in all the preceding thousands. The problems of physical science, however, are the simplest and easiest. Those of biological science are more complex and more difficult, those of social science still more so. These sciences are therefore not so far advanced. But philosophy, I believe, is still for the most part at a stage of potential development not very different from the stage that had been reached in Bacon's time by the natural sciences, whose earlier procedures he condemned. Only now is philosophy showing signs of beginning to emerge from its period of blind groping.

Which of its problems are genuine and which illusory, and what are the methods by which solutions of those that are genuine may be reached, are questions which indeed have arisen more than once in the past, but to which more attention is being given at present than perhaps ever before. The time seems at hand when an answer more convincing than any previously offered may be possible. The present volume constitutes an attempt to shed upon these questions such light as the writer believes he perceives.

A number of recent contentions concerning the nature of philosophy and its proper method which seem unsound will first be reviewed and criticized. The second part of the book will outline the answers proposed by the writer to these two questions.

PART I

Some Recent Hypotheses as to the
Nature and Method of Philosophy

CHAPTER ONE

Philosophy as More General than Science

O NE of the criteria most frequently offered by philosophers themselves, when asked what distinguishes philosophy from science, is that philosophy deals with questions more general in character than those of the sciences. Exactly what this means, however, is hardly ever made very clear. Let us examine some of the meanings in which the assertion may be construed.

1. *Philosophy as a Synthetic Picture of the World as a Whole.*—One interpretation would be that philosophy "deals with those most general truths which do not belong to the field of any special science," each of the special sciences being "concerned only with particular features and parts of the great whole," while philosophy aims at "a general world-view in which all the different truths of the special sciences find their places and are unified into one great picture."[1] The relation between the sciences and philosophy is thus conceived as analogous to that between the pieces of a jigsaw puzzle and the coherent picture they make when

---

[1] Schlick, *op. cit.*, p. 51. This view is not Schlick's own, but his formulation is quoted because it is both brief and quite faithful to the conception of philosophy it represents.

properly assembled. The picture, let us say, might be that of a man; the separate pieces might be one a representation of an eye, another of an ear, another of an arm, a leg, etc. Each of the sciences puts together its part out of original smaller pieces, and philosophy then assembles these parts into the picture of the whole man.

This metaphor, describing philosophy as it does in terms of a very clear and familiar relation, seems illuminating and is quite plausible until one asks what literally are the facts that it figuratively describes. In just what sense does philosophy "unify" or "put together," for instance, physics and biology, or biology and psychology? What answers we actually get from philosophers on such a question as that of the relation of physics and biology are opinions as to whether "life" is explicable purely in terms of physics and chemistry, or, on the contrary, constitutes an additional principle. Facts bearing on this question—as distinguished from guesses—are brought forward only by persons who have a technical knowledge of biology and of physical science, whether or not they are trained in philosophy. It is biologists like D'Arcy W. Thompson, or physicists like N. Rashevsky, and not metaphysicians, who point out, and alone are in a position to point out, the similarity between the pattern of cell division in the realm of biology and the pattern of aggregation of soap bubbles in the realm of physics, and the conformity of both these patterns to one common set of abstract physical and mathematical principles. Moreover, although what is thus brought to light is the essential unity in this respect of certain biological and physical phenomena, the synthesis effected does not have title to the name of philosophy.

On such a question as that of the relation of the truths of physics to those of biology, philosophers *qua* philosophers simply do not know the facts to be "unified." The "syntheses" of which they deliver themselves have thus actually to do only with such vague current concepts as "life" and "inert matter." They represent not more comprehensive or more penetrating insights than are possible to biologists and physicists, but only either metaphorical statements quickly shown to be empty by any attempt to translate them into literal terms, or else irresponsible and unprecise lay guesses. As M. C. Otto has pointed out, "all-inclusive philosophical systems are not striking in virtue of how much they include, but in virtue of how much they leave out. The difference between them and other selective schemes consists in the nature of what is retained and rejected, and in the purpose that dominates the choices."[2] As will be pointed out in the chapter following, the purpose or criterion that has actually governed the choices required in the construction of all-inclusive world-pictures seems not infrequently to have been the suitability of the resulting world-picture to serve subjectively as a substitute for the knowledge of the universe man yet lacks to make himself secure. A world-picture does not need to be true to serve subjectively as such a substitute. It needs only to be believable and of such a nature that, if firmly believed, it generates in man the subjective feelings of hope and confidence that he craves, and rids him of the fear and bewilderment that go with a consciousness of ignorance as to matters of crucial importance.

2. *Spencer's View of Philosophy as Knowledge of the Highest Generality.*—We may now consider a somewhat different account of what is meant by saying that philosophy is more general than science, viz., the account given by

---

[2] "Meditation on a Hill," *Philosophical Review*, XXXIX, No. 4 (July, 1930), p. 341.

Herbert Spencer.[3] It is worded in less figurative language than most, but just because of this its untenability is the more evident.

Spencer characterizes philosophy as "knowledge of the highest degree of generality," and explains what he means by this with three illustrations. The flow of a river, he points out, is a corollary of the more general facts stated by the laws of the dynamics of fluids. These laws themselves are corollaries of those of general dynamics, which describe how bodies in general—whether fluid or solid—move. Similarly the fact of warm-bloodedness is a corollary, ultimately, of rate of molecular motion. Again, the fact that excess of demand over supply determines price is a corollary of the general fact that man seeks satisfaction for his desires in ways costing the smallest efforts. Spencer goes on to say that "so long as these truths are known only apart and regarded as independent, even the most general of them cannot without laxity of speech be called philosophical." Philosophy is reached "by carrying a stage farther the process indicated," viz., that of generalization:

When, having been severally reduced to a simple mechanical axiom, a principle of molecular physics, and a law of social action, they are contemplated together as corollaries of some ultimate truth, then we rise to the kind of knowledge that constitutes philosophy proper. The truths of philosophy thus bear the same relation to the highest scientific truths that each of these bears to lower scientific truths.[4]

Unfortunately, as pointed out in the preceding section, it

---

[3] *First Principles*, §37.

[4] It may be noted that Spencer's second and third examples, as set forth in detail in his text, do not illustrate the same thing as the first, viz., the description of a given fact successively in terms of more and more general laws. The second illustrates successive corrections of the hasty generalization that breathing causes hot-bloodedness, and the third presents several facts as all of them corollaries of one generalization.

is in vain that we seek, among the truths or alleged truths of metaphysics or other branches of philosophy, for any laws under which the laws of mechanics, of molecular physics, and of social action could all be subsumed and from which they could each be deduced, in the same sense in which the laws of the dynamics of fluids can be subsumed under and deduced from those of general dynamics. Moreover, metaphysical generalizations, e.g., those that describe the world as being essentially material, or essentially mental, etc., have to those of any science a relation quite other than that which the more inclusive generalizations of one science have to its less inclusive ones. This is shown by the fact that philosophical materialism and philosophical idealism, although regarded as mutually incompatible, are, nevertheless, equally compatible with all the facts discovered by the natural sciences. They are compatible with them because, whereas the generalizations of natural science, even the very widest, provide a basis for the prediction of certain facts in nature, those philosophical generalizations do not claim to do this but only to "interpret"—in some none too well defined sense of this term—the facts described by the generalizations of the natural sciences.

Thus, it is simply not true that philosophy is more general than natural science in the sense that it carries farther the generalizing of the same facts. The generalizations which science formulates concerning the facts it observes are carried by it just as far as the facts themselves permit. The scientist does not hesitate to cross the boundaries—which actually consist of nothing more permanent than ignorance—between the subject matter of two sciences, if he finds himself able to state a true generalization applicable to both. Never do his descriptions of the facts he observes reach a degree of generality where, for lack of adequate powers of generalization, he finds that he has to leave further generalization to some Herr Teufelsdroeckh, professor of things-in-general!

Nor is philosophy more general than science in the sense that, in its own domain, it carries generalization farther than does natural science in the domain it investigates. Philosophy, like science, deals with some questions that are highly specific and with some that are highly general. Like science, it has its special divisions, perhaps connected, but susceptible, like the special sciences, of being studied more or less independently of one another. The fact is that the questions philosophy asks are not essentially either more or less general than those which science asks, but simply different. Philosophy is curious about something else.

3. *Origin of the Opinion that Philosophy is More General than Science.*—The mistaken opinion that philosophy is "more general" than science is accounted for by two considerations. One of these is that the propositions formulated by philosophers, and especially by the metaphysicians, have very often been extremely vague, and the logical connections between them, or with known facts, correspondingly hard to discern. It is very easy to mistake ambiguity for generality, indefiniteness for abstractness, and absence of logical connection for depth or subtlety of connection.

The other consideration is that knowledge is one of the things philosophy studies, and that the sciences seem describable as constituting each a particular species of knowledge. When one adverts to this, it sounds very plausible to say that the branch of philosophy which studies knowledge studies something more general than any of the sciences. But such a conclusion springs only from confusion between knowledge in the sense of *knowing* and knowledge in the sense of *facts known*. The various sciences constitute not various species

of knowing, but the knowing of various species of facts.
What the philosopher, *qua* epistemologist, studies is thus
not at all the same facts as the scientist studies, at a more
general level, but the quite other fact constituted by the
nature of the relation, called knowing, which the scientist
is attempting to establish between himself and the facts he
studies. The physicist, for example, seeks to know the nature
of the physical world; but the epistemologist seeks to know
the nature of the relation, viz., knowing, which the physicist
is seeking to establish between himself and the physical
world.

4. *Philosophy as Harmonizer of Religion and Science.*—
A somewhat different and more restricted, yet allied, view
of the task of philosophy is that it consists in harmonizing
the truths of religion and those of natural science. But, as
S. K. Langer pointedly observes, "despite the hundreds of
books that have been written in the past two or three centuries seeking to reconcile theology with biology, divine
law with natural law, and angels with anthropoids, philosophy has neither softened the conflict of ideas nor dictated
the peace."[5] In any case, philosophy in general could not
possibly be defined as the attempt to perform that task, for
much of philosophy deals with quite other matters.

5. *Philosophy as Potential Natural Science.*—There is
another conception of the nature of philosophy which
resembles some of those above discussed, at least in that it
too regards philosophy as a stage of science—not, however,
the stage of completion, but rather that at which science is
yet infantile. According to this view, which, Langer points

---
[5] *The Practice of Philosophy* (1930), p. 8.

out, apparently was the one held by William James, philosophy is essentially "potential natural science." In James's own words, it is "a collective name for questions that have not yet been answered to the satisfaction of all by whom they have been asked."[6]

More explicitly, this means that if the questions James refers to are essentially of the same sort as those which natural science asks and answers little by little, then philosophy is a name not for the study of any distinctive subject matter, but only for a distinguishable stage in the study of any question concerning nature. As Langer remarks, philosophers could then be described only as "dilettantes, interested laymen asking questions out of order, ever anticipating the expert's consistent, progressive exposition"; and philosophy itself would accordingly be merely "the Art of Making Hasty Generalizations."[7]

Philosophers, especially cosmologists, have, it is true, only too often themselves mistaken the proper subject matter of philosophy, and been led thus to deliver themselves of opinions, relating to certain scientific questions, that were indeed nothing but hasty generalizations. But these mistakes of philosophers are no more representative of the nature of philosophy than the equally hasty statements of Millikan or Einstein concerning God, or of Eddington concerning the relation of reality to mind, are representative of the nature of science.

The assertion that philosophy is only potential natural science is generally based on the historical fact that early thinkers, who were called philosophers, explored subjects some of which, when they became sufficiently developed, acquired names and exclusive devotees of their own, and

---

[6] *Some Problems of Philosophy*, p. 23.
[7] *Op. cit.*, pp. 10, 12.

from then on led existences independent of the parent mass, which kept the name of philosophy. When this process is completed, it is argued, philosophy will automatically vanish for lack of subject matter distinct from that of the several sciences.

But the fact that in early times the various fields of knowledge were not clearly distinguished, and that not only then but even until not so long ago anyone who sought knowledge for its own sake, no matter on what subject, was called a philosopher, constitutes no evidence whatever that the studies which have given up the name of philosophy do not, in subject matter, differ from philosophy as radically as does mathematics from the natural sciences.

So long as the process of separation of the sciences from the philosophical "mother" has not actually resulted in the vanishing of philosophy, the assertion that that process will leave no final remainder, i.e., that philosophy does not have a subject matter distinct from that of the sciences, remains only a dogma. And it is a strange one indeed to base, as it usually is based, on the metaphorical description of philosophy as the mother of the sciences. For what the metaphor implies—for whatever it is worth—is not that a mother consists of nothing but the children growing in her womb, but only that her own individual nature is such as to fit her to nourish them in their embryonic and infant stages. Metaphors, however, really constitute no evidence, whichever way they point. That philosophy has a subject matter of its own, distinct from that of both the natural and the formal sciences, can be established only by pointing out explicitly what this consists in. The attempt to do this will be made in the second part of the present volume.

CHAPTER TWO

Philosophy as Logically Articulated Faith

IN THE preceding chapter, we considered the contention that philosophy has the same subject matter as science, but seeks not merely partial but all-inclusive generalizations concerning it. The positive ground upon which disagreement with that contention was based was that although it is temptingly plausible, nevertheless the difference between philosophy and science is really not of this kind, but is a difference in the nature of the facts that each investigates, i.e., a difference of subject matter.

1. *Is there a Philosophical Method Distinct from the Scientific?*—The synoptic views or world-interpretations that philosophers have formulated indeed represent attempted generalizations, but concerning philosophy's own subject matter—generalizations, that is, not continuous with and different only in degree from those of science, but rather concerned with facts quite other than those which the natural or the formal sciences study.

Notwithstanding this, the contrast earlier mentioned between the evident progress of science and the apparent lack of comparable progress in philosophy remains glaring.

It has led various writers to urge upon philosophy the need of becoming scientific in method; and this has focused interest on the question whether, since philosophy and science do address themselves to different problems, the methods of science are at all appropriate to philosophy. Is it not perhaps the case that progress in philosophy means something different from progress in science—that, in its own direction, philosophy has equally progressed, and that it has a method of its own as appropriate to its problems as scientific method is to those of the sciences? We shall in this chapter consider a recent attempt to vindicate philosophy along the lines suggested by this question.

2. *Hoernlé's View of the Nature of Philosophy.*—In an essay on "The Philosopher's Quest"[1] Hoernlé, after reviewing the criticisms to which philosophy has lately been subjected, asks what a philosopher can do to reassure himself concerning the nature and value of philosophy. He suggests that the answer must be found in advertence to the nature and value not so much of philosophy as of the spontaneous activity called philosophizing.

The essential spirit of that activity, he tells us, is "the spirit of wholeness": to philosophize "is to seek an attitude towards the universe as a whole." However, since the whole universe cannot be presented to our thought, "wholeness is not to be understood quantitatively, but qualitatively. It consists, at the very least, in that quality of *organization* in virtue of which alone we can say that we experience a 'universe,' or live in a 'world.' Order, correlation of differences, system, are aspects of it, or forms of it." Our experiences, that is to say, exhibit some order and connection,

---

[1] *Op. cit.*

and more of this may be discovered in them by reflection. That orderliness and connectedness are a character of the universe is a lesson that experience itself can teach us; and "to philosophise is nothing but the sustained attempt to elicit this lesson." Objects and experiences are thus the data or materials for philosophizing, which itself is rather "the effort at synthesis, or synopsis, which acknowledges at bottom but one 'object'—call it, as we will, reality, God, the absolute, the universe, the whole." And the "stability in thought and feeling and action" that perception of the wholeness of the universe brings constitutes wisdom, which is the goal of philosophizing.

3. *Is Philosophizing Only Wishful Thinking?*—The objection that philosophizing is then only a species of wishful thinking immediately suggests itself, and is stated by Hoernlé himself with great clarity as a preliminary to the attempt he makes to dispose of it. The objection, as he phrases it, is that wholeness is predicable "not of the universe as a fact, but only of the philosopher's point of view as an aspiration; that it means wholeness of attitude rather than attitude towards a whole; that it is subjective and psychological, not objective and metaphysical; an intellectual demand or ideal, not an actual, or at least not a verifiable, character of the nature of things." For the universe, "as it comes to us in experience . . . . is sufficiently chaotic to stamp the suggestion of its all-pervading orderliness as, at best, an hypothesis . . . . for thought and conduct, not an objective truth," or else as "an escape from intolerable actualities into the purer world of imagination."

In considering this objection, Hoernlé not only fully admits, but insists, that philosophy cannot be justified by its subjective satisfactoriness if the dualism of objective chaos and subjective orderliness remains: "a unified life is possible only in a unified world; in a cosmos, not in a chaos." Moreover, the philosopher's organization of experience is not successful unless the order that it displays is inherent in experience. Yet, by way of dealing with the objection he has so clearly stated, Hoernlé offers remarks that only postulate what needed to be shown. To call attention to this postulative character in the passages I now quote, I have italicized in each case the word from the use of which that character arises. Hoernlé says, for example, that "*unless* the universe is a whole, it is meaningless to talk of seeking an attitude towards it as a whole"; that the phrase "the point of view of the whole" *means* "that the conviction of the wholeness of the universe is a lesson of experience, is taught us by the logic of the facts." That phrase, he says, "*claims* that experiences, drawn together by reflection, focused so as to interpret each other and thus reveal their common and total meaning, supply the evidence which justifies the conviction of unity and order." And philosophizing, he concludes, "is the pursuit of a will-o'-the-wisp, unless the philosopher can rely on the principle that there is nothing in the whole range of experience which does not, in its own degree and measure, help to reveal the nature of the universe."

Let us admit, indeed insist, that the philosopher can and must rely on that principle. What then does reliance upon it reveal to him as to the nature of the universe? That it is a unitary, orderly whole? No. For the objection to the original assertion that it is such a whole was precisely that the universe "as it comes to us in experience . . . is sufficiently chaotic to stamp the suggestion of its all-pervading orderliness as, at best, an hypothesis." It is true that Hoernlé says that the appeal to experience "requires an openness of mind which, whilst rejecting no evidence, relies with due discrimination on the most significant and illuminating experiences." But what does it mean to say that certain experiences are "most significant and illuminating," except that they are experiences which support the conclusion we desire to reach? If one is thus allowed to rule out as not significant any experience which testifies against one's contention, then one can prove practically any contention.

The fact that what experience does reveal is some order indeed, but also some chaos, remains an insuperable objection to defining philosophy initially, as Hoernlé proposes, as the attempt to show that the object of our experience is a whole, a universe and not a "multiverse." For this, after all, is not a definition of philosophy but only the *thesis* of one kind of philosophy, viz., the monistic. Philosophizing, or, more specifically, metaphysics, has not consisted only in attempting to show that the monistic thesis is true, but rather in attempting to discover which thesis is true, the monistic or the pluralistic, the idealistic or the naturalistic, etc., or whether any of them is true. Often, indeed, some form of unity can, upon investigation, be discerned in apparent disunity, but sometimes what study discovers is disunity behind apparent unity. At all events, no matter how numerous may be the instances where some unity or orderliness has been discovered in what previously seemed a chaotic set of facts, the belief that orderliness and unity completely pervade the world of our experience represents not a known fact but only a fond hope, so long as there remain any unresolved disunities in it. Countless ones do remain.

4. *The Search for Unity No Guarantee that Unity Exists.*—Effort at synthesis, it should be noted, is not distinctive of philosophy. Philosophy also seeks to analyze; and synthesis

is no less a part of the effort of science. Both philosophy and science seek unities, regularities, characters that remain invariant through given ranges of variation. As pointed out in the preceding chapter, only the nature of the ranges each explores differentiates the two. Even if philosophy or the sciences were interested only in and looked for nothing but the "pearls" which unities in diversity constitute, and could therefore be defined as consisting of the search for them, this would not in the least guarantee the presence of such a pearl in every oyster. A philosopher whose effort at synthesis "acknowledges at bottom but one 'object' . . . . the whole" is like a pearl diver who should decide to "acknowledge" only oysters containing pearls. Or, if "acknowledging" means only "being satisfied by," there is no a priori or a posteriori reason to believe that what exists is exactly what it would need to be to satisfy us. The complete orderliness some of us crave and persistently seek in the world may not be there, or, even if it is, may be so recondite as forever to elude discernment by the mind of man. This would mean that it must remain forever indistinguishable from a partial chaos, and can no more than the latter constitute the basis for a wisdom.

Refusal to "acknowledge" chaos, or anything else, is an incongruous gesture if what one is engaged in is the search for objective truth. That gesture can be congruous only to something very different, viz., to the selection, from among the various features of the world we find, of one of them as most interesting or most valuable to us, and therefore as the one for which, to the neglect of all others, or in preference to any other, we resolve to search everywhere. Monism, thus, although it cannot be put forth as a verifiable description of the facts we find, can be put forth as a definition of a position we propose to take, i.e., as a definition of the difference between what we shall prize as satisfying to us and what we shall pass over as unsatisfying.

5. *Metaphysical Syntheses Worthless when Only Verbal.*— Aside from this, however, it is essential that such syntheses as are effected shall not, as too often in metaphysics, be merely verbal syntheses. For to explain what we do not understand by saying—perhaps in highly esoteric language and at great length—that God does it, or to harmonize conflicts by saying, perhaps, that they are reconciled and transcended in the consciousness of the Absolute, is not really but only verbally to explain and to harmonize. It is but to give some august proper name to the solution which we hope exists for our difficulties, and to mistake familiarity with the proper name for knowledge of the solution. No explanation or reconciliation of known facts in terms of some postulated entity is real explanation or reconciliation, nor is it any ground for belief that the postulated entity exists, unless the supposition that it exists makes possible inferences which facts not yet known verify when known, *and* unless these inferences are at least in part different from those that would be possible if an entity different from the one postulated existed in its stead. Unfortunately, most metaphysicians apply these tests of the not merely verbal character of any speculative construction either not at all or only haphazardly to their speculative constructions. This is perhaps because it has not been clear to them what an empirical test of the truth of these constructions might consist in.

6. *Hoernlé on Philosophical Method.*—What conception of philosophical method, we may now ask, accompanies Hoernlé's view of the nature of philosophy and philosophizing discussed above? What he has to say of a positive rather

than of a critical sort on the subject appears to stem from
his fundamental agreement with James's statement, which he
quotes, that philosophies are "just so many visions, modes
of feeling the whole push, and seeing the whole drift of life,"
and that these visions are "forced on one by one's total
character and experience, and on the whole *preferred* . . . . as
one's best working attitude." For the basis of philosophy in
vision or insight means "that philosophical argument of the
best sort is *material*, not formal."² Therefore, although "philosophers have again and again pinned their hopes to some
reform in method," the salvation of philosophy will not
be brought about by this alone: "unless the material quality
of the would-be philosopher's data be of the right sort, skill
in dialectics will not give him the fundamental insights."
Hoernlé accordingly has little of a positive nature to contribute to the problem of philosophical method. We find him
saying only such things as that "there is a weighing of
considerations, a trying out of alternatives, a mobilizing of
all the resources of one's experiences and reflection, a feeling
one's way from a distracted and unstable to a coherent and
stable outlook." The philosopher, he adds, may not be able
to demonstrate to others the conclusions he reaches in this
way, "for demonstration requires not merely technical
correctness of the argument, but acceptance by the other of
its premises." These, however, are held by Hoernlé to
"depend on the range and quality of each thinker's concrete
experience," but in a sense, apparently, in which the premises
of arguments in science are not similarly dependent. However,
although demonstration of one's philosophical theory may
thus be impossible, "yet a reasoned and reasonable theory

---

² Hoernlé, *op. cit.*, chap. ii, p. 27. The quotations that follow are from the same
chapter.

(or, if the word be preferred, 'faith') is not unattainable and has rewarded the venture of philosophizing again and again."

7. *Philosophy as the Articulation of a Faith.*—What perhaps throws most light upon Hoernlés view of philosophy and its method is the description, in the passage just quoted, of philosophies as *faiths*, implied also when he writes: "There is a deep-seated need in the human mind . . . . the need to feel at home in the universe. From this source spring all philosophies and all religions. . . . . It is a need which at once demands to understand the universe and to approve—nay, to love it."[3]

These passages make clear that, according to Hoernlé, what philosophizing seeks is not really knowledge but logically articulated faith, that is, not conclusions susceptible of being demonstrated, but only conclusions susceptible of being believed by a rational being. And, let it be carefully noted, the believability to a rational, i.e., logical being, of a set of propositions about the universe (especially if they be very abstract), does not require that they be true but only that they be free from manifest contradictions, and have bearing on the given individual's spiritual problems.

This remark, I believe, largely explains the emphasis which idealistic philosophy especially, in its metaphysical constructions, has tended to lay on system, consistency, and coherence as criteria, and its accompanying neglect of the question of the truth (as something distinct from coherence) of those constructions. Both the emphasis and the neglect are explained by the hypothesis that what was being sought through those metaphysical constructions was, unconsciously rather than consciously, not fundamentally knowledge con-

---

[3] *Idealism as a Philosophy*, p. 23.

cerning man's relation to the universe, but only a believable conceptual content for a faith about that relation.

8. *Philosophy and Religion.*—It may be readily admitted that metaphysical systems, whether their propositions be true or not, can be and have widely been used as just such more or less easily believable contents for faiths about the relation between man and the world—as substitutes for the dogmas of revealed religions—by persons who found themselves unable to believe the latter and yet craved something to believe. But construction of a believable set of dogmas articulating an unrevealed, man-made religion is nevertheless something between which and philosophy there remains the difference that subsists between faith and knowledge. Belief is knowledge when it has adverted to the evidence and goes no farther than the latter warrants; it is on the contrary faith when it neglects the evidence or goes beyond it. To make this distinction sharp is not to disparage faith or to suggest that it has no legitimate function in the life of man. It is only to make clear the meaning of the question as to which of the two—faith or knowledge—philosophy seeks to be. It seems to me beyond question that what most philosophers have considered themselves engaged in was the pursuit of knowledge properly so called. And Hoernlé himself seems to agree that this is what philosophy seeks, when he insists that its conclusions must be dictated "by the logic of the facts"—by what experience reveals. Yet he ends by characterizing philosophy as faith, and as born of the need to understand, to approve, and to love the universe.

But philosophy cannot essentially be both together. Which of the two it is turns on the answer to the question: What ultimately ought to determine the nature of the conclusions of philosophy? Ought it to be the human craving

to understand, approve, and love the universe? Or ought it
to be faithfulness to the testimony of the observable facts,
even if this testimony should be that the universe is chaotic,
blameworthy, and hateful? The need to choose between these
two imperatives would never arise if both always dictated
the same conclusions. In any case, it is the choice we are
prepared to make between the two, if we have to choose,
that answers the question as to whether what we expect the
conclusions of our thinking to provide is essentially a comforting religious faith, or philosophical knowledge.

9. *Urban's Conception of Philosophy Open to Similar
Criticisms.*—Comments of the same general nature as those
applying to Hoernlé's conception of the nature of philosophy
seem to me relevant to W. M. Urban's defense of the "great
tradition" in philosophy, which, he says, is characterized
by the fact that it finds the world "ultimately meaningful
and intelligible."[4] For to evaluate the soundness of any
enterprise which purports to be a search for truth not yet
known, on the basis of whether what it discovers is of a
kind we welcome rather than abhor, is to confess that what
we are interested in is essentially comforting belief rather
than truth. Even if, as Hoernlé and Urban hold, truth and
comforting belief should happen to coincide—thus saving
us from the necessity of actually deciding which we value
most—nevertheless, as remarked above, what is significant
of the sort of enterprise we are really engaged in is which of
the two we are ready to choose if the necessity for choice
between them should present itself. I hold that unless truth
is what we are prepared to cling to in any such case, our
enterprise is not really philosophy but religion incognito.

---

[4] *The Intelligible World* (1929), p. 1.

If this is admitted to be the test of genuinely philosophical enterprise, then the test cannot be what kind of world we find as a result of genuine philosophizing.

That these remarks are relevant to Urban's position will become evident if we now note what he has to say on the subject of intelligibility. He makes clear what he means when he contrasts knowledge of the world, which the sciences give us, with understanding of it, which they do not give us but which philosophy should, and tells us that by understanding he means axiological interpretation: "If genuine intelligibility is sought, the essential function of philosophy must become axiological interpretation, and it is at this point that the distinctive ideal of philosophical intelligibility is to be found."[5]

In the light of this passage, Urban's statement that "in the last resort there are only two kinds of philosophies: those that find the world ultimately meaningful and intelligible and those that do not," means that the former—those belonging to the "great tradition"—find the world axiologically interpretable, and the latter—the "modernist"— do not. But one is moved to ask whether any philosophies exist that do not find the world axiologically interpretable. Bertrand Russell's philosophy, for instance, is beyond doubt regarded by Urban as being in anything but the "great tradition"—rather as an example, if not the most horrible example, of "modernism" in philosophy. Yet it certainly does not find the world axiologically uninterpretable. As Hoernlé has pointed out, it concludes with a very definite evaluation of the world when it asserts the concrete part of it, at least, to be such that reason cannot be at home in it, such that it denies the hopes and the ideals of man, and

---

[5] *Op. cit.*, p. 180, note.

therefore calls for stoicism or for a retreat into the serene abstract realm of mathematics and logic.

This makes it clear that when Urban speaks of finding the world intelligible, he means not merely finding it axiologically interpretable, but in addition and essentially finding it interpretable in a way satisfying to the aspirations of man. That is, he gratuitously identifies value with what is only a species of value, viz., positive as distinguished from negative value:

> The world, to be intelligible . . . . must be *livable*. . . . . An intelligible world is . . . . in the last analysis one in which a life of meaning and significance can be lived. In a world ultimately impenetrable, ultimately incomprehensible, such a life is, indeed, impossible. But what makes a penetrable, a comprehensible world? Is it not finally and solely the fact that it provides the context for an intelligible life? Any life, to be intelligible, requires to be understood through the ideals or values by which that life is lived. But a world, in order to be an intelligible context for such a life, must also be one in which the values, by which the individual life is lived, have their counterpart in an order of values that is cosmic.[6]

But obviously a life lived in terms of fear, bewilderment, disappointed hopes, and stoical resignation or psychological escape, is, alas, only too intelligible to us; for most of us have had some taste of life in such terms. And the world which is an intelligible context for such a life must indeed be one in which the values by which the individual life is lived have their counterpart in a certain aspect of a cosmic order of values, but in this case a negative aspect, viz., an order which includes danger, unintelligibility, ruthlessness, inexorability.

Urban seems constantly to be assuming that the fact that we seek something—specifically, intelligibility—presupposes

---

[6] *Ibid.*, p. 183.

that it is present where we seek it. But what is true is only that any conscious seeking presupposes that we know what sort of thing it is that we seek. That is, seeking something does not presuppose either that we know it to exist, or that it does exist. The conscious search for intelligibility presupposes existence in us of knowledge of what intelligibility would consist in; but that is something very different from knowledge of the existence of intelligibility in the world outside us. Knowing what we are looking for does not prove or create the slightest presumption that it exists.[7] Existence of a thought is not existence of the matter thought of. The latter alone is here in question.

10. *Urban on Philosophical Method.*—The great instrument of philosophical discovery, according to Urban, is the "principle of self-refutation." It "has always been the favourite method of distinguishing between" necessary presuppositions of intelligible philosophical discourse, and mere avoidable prejudices of this or that philosopher—"it may almost be said to be the typical philosophical method."[8]

I do not believe, however, that Urban anywhere describes in general terms how exactly the principle of self-refutation operates in proving that a given proposition has the status of necessary presupposition of intelligible discourse. What he does is to describe in some detail one example of self-refutation, viz., that of a skeptic who happens to assert that he knows nothing. But he does not point out which proposition in particular is shown to be a "presupposition of intelligible discourse" rather than an "avoidable prejudice" by the fact that the skeptic's assertion is self-refuting. As concerns the question of the work which the principle "may

[7] Cf. Aristotle *Analyt. post.* ii, chap. 7.
[8] *Op. cit.*, p. 44.

legitimately be expected to perform," Urban indicates his intention of showing it in detail farther on, and for the time says that "it *is one of the determining principles of intelligible philosophical discourse.* It is concerned with those presuppositions which the thinker cannot deny without making himself unintelligible."[9]

Let us see first what is the case of Urban's skeptic. He is supposed to have asserted with conviction that he knows nothing. If it is true that he knows nothing, he then does not even know that he knows nothing; and yet to have asserted that he knows nothing was to claim that he knew that. Therefore, "this which he claims to know he does not know."[10]

It may be remarked first that if, as supposedly was the case, all that the skeptic did was to assert with conviction, "I do not know anything," then he has not refuted himself. For he has not either asserted or implied that he knows that he does not know anything. What he delivered himself of was only a statement of something he believes, and the proposition he believes, viz., "I do not know anything," not only may be true but may without contradiction be believed by him. For to believe the truth is not the same thing as to know the truth. Yet to believe the proposition, "I do not know anything," is genuinely to be a skeptic, or at least an agnostic.

However, the case Urban means to consider is evidently that of a person who not only is a skeptic in that he believes the proposition, "I do not know anything," but in addition has been foolish enough to assert also, "I know that I do not know anything." Now this assertion, containing as it does a contradiction, is of course false a priori and self-refut-

---

[9] *Ibid.*, p. 46.
[10] *Ibid.*, p. 45.

ing. The contradictory of it is therefore true a priori and self-evident. That contradictory is, "Either I know something, or I do not know that I do not know anything," which is a special case of the principle of excluded middle. Urban states that from the fact that the skeptic has contradicted himself, one cannot conclude that he knows anything; and this is, as just pointed out, quite correct. But what can one then conclude? What, in the instance, has, by appeal to the principle of self-refutation, been shown to be a "necessary presupposition of intelligible discourse?" So far as I can see, nothing at all. The principles of noncontradiction and of excluded middle themselves are statements of certain conditions of the possibility of truth of discourse, or, if we should prefer to call it so, conditions of the material intelligibility of discourse.[11] But even that is not shown by pointing out that the unwary skeptic's assertion was self-contradictory. It is shown by pointing out that pointing out that it is self-contradictory is universally accepted as sufficient evidence that his assertion cannot be true.

In any case, the propositions which, by appeal to the principle of self-refutation, Urban claims to establish as necessary presuppositions of intelligible philosophical discourse, are not the principles of noncontradiction and excluded middle themselves. They are the propositions that the world is a totality, has meaning and value, and is real. But what I find in his text at the crucial points seems to be either an invoking of the principle only in the sense of mentioning it, i.e., without showing how it establishes what it is invoked to establish, or else the forcing upon the assertion alleged to

---

[11] They are not, however, conditions of the formal intelligibility of discourse. For example, the term "round square" implies a contradiction. Yet its meaning is so clearly intelligible to me that if any figure be drawn, I can immediately tell whether or not it is a round square, and why it is or is not.

be self-refuting—which he supposes to be made by some one
to disprove the totality, meaningfulness, or reality of the
world—of a meaning obviously other than that which anyone
making that assertion would acknowledge as his own. For
example, he writes: "He who says there is no meaning in the
world is asserting a self-refuting proposition. . . . . He who
says we do not find meaning in the world but put it there is
talking nonsense. For we are in the world and our meanings
are already part of that world."[12]

But who is there, who has said that there is no meaning
in the world, who would acknowledge that what is refuted
by the remarks just quoted is what he meant by what he said?
Obviously, what anyone would mean, who asserted that there
is no meaning in the world, would be that there is none in the
nonhuman or nonanimal world. The world he would be
talking about would not be the world constituted by purposive
beings already known to him to exist. It would be the world,
other than the one they constitute, which they face. What
he would mean would be, for example, that rain, sunshine,
humidity, drought, floods, earthquakes, heat, cold, plagues,
the abundance of the tropics, the revolutions of the planets,
storms and fair weather, the abundance or scarcity of certain
minerals, their distribution, etc.—in short, the other than
man- or animal-made conditions under which man and the
other known purposive animals have to live—are not mani-
festations of purpose, i.e., of a striving for value, on the part
of the rest of the universe. This assertion, whether in fact it
happens to be true or not, is not self-refuting. Moreover, the
question whether that assertion is true is the question men
have in mind when they ask whether there is a God or
whether on the contrary the world they face is only a com-

---

[12] *Op. cit.*, p. 59.

plex of blind mechanical forces. The reply that Urban, in the passage above, makes to men who want to know that, is that they themselves are in the world, and that, since they contain some godliness, the world obviously contains some; and therefore their doubt is self-refuting. This is like saying to a man who has come to a dry goods store, and who asks whether there is in the store any cloth like a sample he brings, that of course there is some, namely his sample, since he is in the store; and that therefore his question is absurd.

CHAPTER THREE

Philosophy as Poetic Literature
about the Cosmos

THE problem of philosophical method has aroused the interest of many philosophers, but most of those who have discussed it have done so only incidentally. Some years ago, however, the late R. G. Collingwood devoted to it, and to the question of the nature of philosophy, an entire volume.[1] The attempt he makes to differentiate philosophy from science, and to vindicate philosophy of the charges of looseness and confusion so often brought against it, is noteworthy for its unusual elaboration, its systematic character, and its high literary quality. But, as I shall try to show, the attempt nevertheless completely fails of its purpose. Indeed, it serves only to provide in itself one more example of the very manner of philosophizing against which those charges are brought. Moreover, the conception of philosophical method Collingwood sets forth is no more defensible than the untenable positions upon which he rests it.

1. *Collingwood's Vindication of Traditional Philosophy.*— Collingwood attempts to define for philosophy a procedure distinct from that of science, and allegedly grounded in the very nature of philosophical concepts. An understanding of

---

[1] *Philosophical Method* (1933).

this procedure, he believes, will vindicate philosophy of the charge that it is loose and confused as compared with science. Before examining that procedure, let us briefly note the nature of the supposed vindication. It is set forth in the following passage:

> To a person who does not understand what philosophy is, or by what processes it moves, the history of those sixty generations [of European philosophical thought] appears as a chaos. . . . . But this appearance of irrationality, I make bold to say, cannot survive the discovery that philosophical thought has a structure of its own, and the hypothesis that in its changes it is obeying the laws of that structure.[2]

Now, even without agreeing with Collingwood that philosophical tradition (except on the assumption he puts forward) is "only a chaos of discordant ravings,"[3] one may nevertheless insist that ravings may well be systematic without ceasing to be ravings. To discover that the thought of the insane has (to apply to it the words he applies to that of philosophers), "a structure of its own, and . . . . that in its changes it is obeying the laws of that structure," is not to discover that it is after all not insane thought. It is only to discover the laws of the psychology of the insane.

Hence, even if it could be granted that philosophers have typically thought in the way Collingwood describes, no light would thereby be thrown on the merits of that way of thinking. What the nature of that way is, and whether the results it produces are themselves good, are distinct questions. Collingwood's "vindication" of traditional philosophy in effect consists in telling us that the philosophical pudding tastes very bad, unless one knows the recipe by which it was cooked! Yet that it is the taste of the pudding which really decides the merits of the recipe, is his implicit admission

---

[2] *Op. cit.*, p. 224.
[3] *Ibid.*, p. 225.

when in the end he rests his case on the question whether we are willing to believe "that in sixty generations of continuous thought, philosophers have been exerting themselves wholly in vain."[4]

2. *Differentiation of Philosophical and Scientific Concepts.*— Although Collingwood's pages are throughout haunted by the assumption that the question *quid facti* somehow decides the question *quid juris*, much the major portion of his essay consists of an attempt to show that, where philosophical concepts are concerned, the manner in which he alleges philosophers have typically thought is also the manner essentially right. It is this attempt that we must now examine in some detail, for this, if successful, would constitute a genuine vindication of the kind of philosophizing he wishes to defend and of the precepts of philosophical method he lays down. Let us first outline his argument.

Collingwood contends that the difference between the procedures of traditional philosophy and those of science is not evidence of defectiveness in the former, but arises from certain differences between the logical properties of philosophical and of scientific concepts. One of these alleged differences in particular is of such fundamental character that he rests the whole structure as well as the conclusions of his essay upon it. It is, namely, that whereas in scientific concepts the species of a genus are mutually exclusive, in philosophical concepts the species of a genus on the contrary overlap. Collingwood further contends that the species of a philosophical genus constitute a "scale of forms," and, as a result of the alleged overlapping, a scale of a peculiar sort.

A scale of forms arises when differences in degree are combined with differences of kind. For example, in the realm of

---

[4] *Ibid.*

science, differences in the degree of heat of H_2O are accompanied, at certain critical points, by the several kinds of phenomena called ice, water, steam. But in philosophical as distinguished from any scientific scales of forms, the differences of degree are, Collingwood contends, essentially unmeasurable because they are not simply correlated with, but identical with, differences of kind. Every increase, for instance, in heat as we feel it, is, he asserts, also a change in the kind of feeling we experience:

> From a faint warmth through a decided warmth it passes to a definite heat, first pleasant, then dully painful, then sharply painful. . . . . I can detect as many differences in kind as I can detect differences in degree; and these are not two sets of differences but one single set. . . . . In a philosophical scale there is only one set of differences having this peculiar double character [viz., degree and kind].[5]

This itself is due, he asserts, to the fact that

> Differences in degree and differences in kind are two species of the genus difference, and in the case of philosophical concepts they must accordingly overlap to form a type of difference partaking of the nature of both . . . . a difference in degree, but not measurable, and a difference in kind, but not susceptible of arrangement in ungraded species; a difference, that is, between various forms in which the generic essence is embodied, which is also a difference in the degree to which these forms embody it.[6]

In philosophical scales of forms, moreover, the two species of relations called distinction and opposition are (again because of the alleged overlapping of philosophical species) asserted by Collingwood to be fused into a single relation. Opposition, in nonphilosophical concepts

is a relation subsisting between a positive term and its own mere

---

[5] *Op. cit.*, p. 72 f.
[6] *Ibid.*, p. 74.

negation or absence. Cold, as understood by the physicist, is the lack of heat. . . . . But cold as we feel it is not mere lack of heat as we feel it, but another feeling with a positive character of its own; yet these are not two distinct feelings merely, but two opposite feelings.[7]

3. *Collingwood's Precepts of Philosophical Method.*—From such premises Collingwood draws his methodological conclusions. Because in philosophy

the species of a genus are not mutually exclusive, no concept can ever come to us as an absolute novelty; we can only come to know better what to some extent we knew already. We therefore never need an absolutely new word for an absolutely new thing. But we do constantly need relatively new words for relatively new things. This demand cannot be satisfied by technical terms.[8]

On the contrary, technical terms, which Collingwood claims are subjects of verbal as distinct from real definition, thwart that demand because of their rigidity and artificiality:

In order to satisfy it, a vocabulary needs two things: groups of words nearly but not quite synonymous, differentiated by shades of meaning which for some purposes can be ignored and for others become important; and single words which, without being definitely equivocal, have various senses distinguished according to the ways in which they are used.[9]

Formal definitions, accordingly, are taboo in philosophy:

Wherever a philosopher uses a term requiring formal definition . . . . the intrusion of a nonliterary element into his language corresponds with the intrusion of a nonphilosophical element into his thought. . . . . The duty of the philosopher as a writer is therefore to avoid the technical vocabulary proper to science, and to choose his words according to the rules of literature. His terminology must

---

[7] *Ibid.*, p. 75.
[8] *Ibid.*, pp. 205 f.
[9] *Ibid.*, p. 206.

have that expressiveness, that flexibility, that dependence upon context, which are the hallmarks of a literary use of words as opposed to a technical use of symbols.[10]

4. *Do the Co-ordinate Species of a Philosophical Genus Overlap?*—What we must now first examine with particular care is the startling contention upon which Collingwood founds his argument at every point, namely, that in the case of philosophical concepts the species of a genus overlap. It is not necessary, however, to consider all the examples which he adduces in the effort to establish it. One or two will serve as a sample of the rest and will show how precarious is philosophizing which in effect proceeds on the doctrine that precision, because it introduces technicality, is a philosophical sin. Collingwood writes:

> Logic distinguishes within the genus thought two species, judgment or proposition and inference. These, as subject matter of separate parts of logical treatises, seem at first sight to be related much as the triangle and the circle are related in elementary geometry; and in that case they would, like the triangle and the circle, be mutually exclusive classes. But they are not mutually exclusive. That it is raining is a judgment; that it is raining because I can hear it is an inference. Of these two statements one includes the other; and it is therefore clear that the specific classes overlap: a judgment may also be an inference, an inference may also be a judgment.[11]

Now, the only point essential to note here is that even if the example did beyond question show that an inference may be a judgment and a judgment an inference, Collingwood's basic contention that overlapping of the species of a genus is what distinguishes philosophical from scientific concepts would not in the least be established thereby. To establish it, he would need to show not merely that judgment and in-

[10] *Op. cit.*, p. 207.
[11] *Ibid.*, p. 36.

ference overlap and are both of them species of the genus "thought," but in addition that they are co-ordinate species of it. For the overlapping of species that are not co-ordinate is a ubiquitous fact, in no way distinctive of philosophical concepts. Polygon and triangle, for instance, overlap, and both are species, although not co-ordinate species, of geometrical figures. Again, red and scarlet, conifer and pine, rodent and rat respectively overlap, and in each case both are species although not co-ordinate species of, respectively, color, tree, animal. Yet the concepts of geometrical figure, color, tree, animal, are not philosophical concepts.

Co-ordinateness of overlapping species of a philosophical genus is thus the only thing that, if it were a fact, would be distinctive. It is therefore the only thing that needed demonstration, and without demonstration of this Collingwood's examples contribute exactly nothing to show that philosophical concepts have logical properties different from those of scientific concepts. That, in a way, he realizes the crucial importance of co-ordinateness, and that the overlapping concepts he instances (although he almost everywhere refers to them only, indefinitely, as species of a philosophical genus) are tacitly claimed to be in all cases co-ordinate species, is indicated by at least one passage, where he says that when a concept is philosophical "the class of its instances overlaps those of its co-ordinate species."[12] Yet in none of the examples he adduces to prove that overlapping of the species of a genus is what distinguishes philosophical from scientific concepts does he even attempt to show that the species he mentions are co-ordinate.

5. *Another Alleged Example of Overlapping Species.*—One more

---

[12] *Ibid.*, p. 35.

case, this one from the field of ethics, will suffice as sample of the sort of evidence upon which the basic contention of Collingwood's essay rests. He writes:

> Actions are commonly divided into classes according as they are done from motives of different kinds: desire, self-interest, duty. . . . . If it could be held that acts done from these different motives fall into separate and mutually exclusive classes, this would greatly ease the task of assigning to each act its true moral worth. But . . . . moral philosophers have always recognized that in fact our motives are often mixed, so that one and the same act may fall into two or even into all three classes. These and similar considerations make it clear that in our ordinary thought about moral questions, whether we call this thought philosophy or common sense, we habitually think in terms of concepts whose specific classes, instead of excluding one another, overlap.[13]

Now it is perfectly true that we may select from the class of actions in general those where desire is a motive, those where self-interest is a motive, those where duty is a motive. It is also true that these selections of actions overlap. It is also true that each of these three selections would commonly be referred to as a class or a species of actions. But the only question that has any bearing here on what the example is intended to establish is whether they are co-ordinate species of actions. As to this, literary language, which according to Collingwood is what the philosopher must use, unfortunately tells us nothing, for "co-ordinate species" is a technical term belonging to logic. Logic, however, tells us that when a class is being divided on the basis of three principles of dichotomy at once the number of co-ordinate species obtained is eight. They would here be: actions done from desire, self-interest, and duty; actions done from desire and self-interest, but not from duty; actions done from desire, but not from self-interest or from duty; etc.

---

[13] *Op. cit.*, pp. 42 f.

Indeed, by introducing degrees of each of the three motives (assuming them to be measurable), we could divide the class of actions into a much larger number of co-ordinate species, but these species still would not overlap. They would on the contrary be mutually exclusive and together exhaustive of the class of actions. Or has Collingwood perhaps a definition of his own, other than the ordinary one, for co-ordinateness? If he has, it is to be regretted that he did not introduce it even despite his own taboo of formal definitions in philosophy. For so long as we adhere to the ordinary meanings of terms, the contention that the co-ordinate species of a philosophical genus overlap is simply the contention that the co-ordinate species of a philosophical genus are not co-ordinate!

Rejection of a contention which essentially consists of this contradiction does not, as he claims, in the least commit us to "throw overboard the whole conception of genus and species";[14] nor does it involve us in "thinking that every concept must have a group of instances to itself."[15] Nor, again, does our division above of actions into mutually exclusive, co-ordinate species, on the basis of the three determining motives, in any way entail that we "must give up thinking at all about" that particular topic of ethical philosophy."[16] On the contrary, it enables us to think about it without confusion.[17]

---

[14] *Ibid.*, p. 37.
[15] *Ibid.*, p. 48.
[16] *Ibid.*, p. 44.
[17] Partial mutual overlapping of two species of a genus (vs. total overlapping of one by the other) is a character indeed absent from classifications which are scientific in form, i.e., logically useful (whether their subject matter be philosophical or natural-scientific). But presence of that character is not something distinctive of any particular kind of concepts. (Consider, for instance, "aquatic animals" and "mammalian animals.") Presence of partial mutual overlapping of species is only a logical defect, to which any purely empirical classification is exposed. It constitutes a logical defect,

6. Collingwood's Basic Contention either Contradictory or False.—
The very foundation of Collingwood's entire theory of
philosophy and philosophical method is now seen to consist
either of the contradiction that the co-ordinate species of a
genus are not mutually exclusive, or of the false proposition
that overlapping of non-co-ordinate species of a genus is
something to be found only in the case of concepts that are
philosophical. This means that the whole ingenious edifice
he erects on that foundation collapses; and the case against
his view of philosophy and philosophical method might
therefore be rested here. Since, however, falsity of premises
does not necessarily imply falsity of conclusion, some of his
secondary contentions, and the methodological precepts he
finally lays down, might nevertheless happen to be sound.
It is therefore necessary to examine at least the more important
of these secondary contentions.

This will at the same time furnish an a posteriori test of
the merits of the methodological principles which Collingwood recommends. For if these are sound, any errors our
examination may reveal should be traceable to violations of
them. Since, however, his own obedience to them is unquestionably faithful, any errors we find will constitute evidence
of the unsoundness of the principles.

*7. Nonaddibility of "Philosophical" Degrees No Evidence of
Essential Unmeasurability.*—The vice which has now been
exposed in Collingwood's initial and most fundamental
contention is the first and most remarkable of the fruits of
the use of those principles. For it is directly traceable to the
lack of precision which Collingwood regards as a requisite

---

whether the subject matter be philosophical or not, because knowledge that a given
thing does, or does not, fall under one concept furnishes no basis for inference as to
whether or not it falls under the other of the two.

of literary quality, and to the consequent ambiguity of language which he dignifies by describing as expressiveness and flexibility. Other fruits of the same sort are to be found at many other points.

Let us first turn to the contention that what distinguishes the scale of forms allegedly constituted by the species of a philosophical genus is that the differences of degree on which a philosophical scale is based are essentially nonmeasurable. Collingwood bases this contention on the fact that these differences of degree cannot be added together to produce a greater, and on the assumption that nonaddibility implies nonmeasurability. This assumption, however, is erroneous.

An example of nonaddible quantities which are nevertheless measurable is that of temperatures. They are measurable, and universally measured, by means of a thermometer, but, although the figures which measure the temperatures of two rooms, say 60° and 70°, can be added, the temperatures themselves cannot in any way be added to yield a third actual temperature which would be measured as 130°.

As concerns Collingwood's own example, viz., feelings of warmth, their nonmeasurability is not, as he assumes, an implication of their nonaddibility, but is due only to the empirical difficulty of correlating them with some fixed scale, whether a scale consisting of some of them (as the scale for measuring length consists of a set of lengths) or one consisting of units of some other sort of quantity (as the scale for measuring temperatures consists of a set of heights of the mercury column in the thermometer tube). Collingwood's other assertion, that observation of the intensity of some bodily function that happened to vary concomitantly with the intensity of pleasure (or, similarly, of the feeling of warmth) would not constitute measurement of it, is explicable only as based on the false assumption that the scale used to measure something needs to be homogeneous with (instead of only correlated with) the thing measured. The falsity of that assumption is sufficiently shown by the fact that temperatures are admittedly measured by heights of mercury, which are nevertheless something heterogeneous to them.[18]

From these considerations, it is evident that the non-measurability of something that observably admits of more and less is never known to us to be an intrinsic character of it. The most we can ever say about such a thing is that we do not at the time know any way of measuring it.

8. *Differences of Kind, even in Philosophy, Not Identical with Differences of Degree.*—Let us next turn to Collingwood's contention that in "philosophical" scales of forms differences of kind are not correlated with but somehow "fused" or identical with differences of degree. None of the examples by which he attempts to establish the existence of differences of this sort in fact illustrates any such difference, and any appearance these examples may have of doing so is due only to the lack of precision in statement which, according to the methodological precepts Collingwood lays down, would constitute a philosophical virtue.

The fact he mentions, for instance,[19] that the feeling of warmth at a given intensity is pleasant and soothing, at another dully painful or exciting, and at another sharply painful, does not mean, as he asserts, that every increase in the heat I feel is (rather than is merely accompanied by) a change in the kind of feeling I experience. For to say that at any intensity the feeling of warmth becomes different in kind from itself would be to say that the intensity at

---

[18] That is to say, Collingwood simply ignores the distinction between "fundamental" and "derived" measurement, and writes as if all measurement were of the fundamental sort. Cf. N. Campbell, *Measurement and Calculations* (1928).

[19] *Op. cit.*, p. 72.

which this occurs is an intensity not of the feeling of warmth, but of some other. That the feeling of warmth at certain intensities is accompanied, e.g , by pleasure, and at other intensities by pain, shows that other feelings, connected with the feeling of warmth, change at certain intensities of the feeling of warmth, but it does not in the least show that the feeling of warmth itself, at any intensity, becomes qualitatively different from itself; nor, as Collingwood would have us believe, that at slight intensities it is only slightly of its own kind! The case of the allegedly "philosophical" feeling of warmth is thus in no relevant respect different from the case of, let us say, the physical substance iron which, at no matter what temperature or pressure, etc., completely remains iron, notwithstanding the diversity of the attributes it exhibits at various temperatures, pressures, etc.

9. *Species of a Genus Never Species of It in Various Degrees.*—Nowhere, in spite of all his efforts, does Collingwood give any evidence whatever that the species of a genus (whether co-ordinate or not) may be species of it in various degrees. What is possible—and, if stated with sufficient lack of precision, might be mistaken for this—is that the individual entities which belong to a given species of a genus should possess the generic character only in a degree too small for some stated purpose. But that degree is never too small, if greater than zero, for the purpose of insuring that the entities of the given species belong as fully as any others to its genus. In the case of academic degrees, for instance, which Collingwood offers as an example, it would obviously be false to say that the lowest, viz., the bachelor's, is only slightly an academic degree. What is true is that the degree of scholarly attainment (not of academic-degree-ness) which this species of academic degree represents is lower than that

represented by the other degrees, and is possibly too low for certain purposes.

10. *Distinction and Opposition, even in Philosophy, Not Fused into a Single Relation.*—Let us finally consider Collingwood's contention that, in philosophical concepts, distinction and opposition are "fused into a single relation." One example he uses is that of the feeling of cold and the distinct but allegedly opposed feeling of warmth. Yet he not only fails to show that the feelings of warmth and of cold are "opposed" to each other, but he even omits to say what would constitute opposition of the "philosophical" sort, as distinguished from the "nonphilosophical" relation "subsisting between a positive term and its own mere negation or absence." He merely asserts that the two feelings, although not opposed in this sense, are yet "opposed." The fact is, however, that the feeling of warmth and the feeling of cold are opposed only each to its own psychological zero. This zero happens, for both, to correspond to a physical temperature about that of the blood, and therefore when a temperature moderately higher or lower than this is applied to one area of the skin— i.e. to one group of cutaneous organs consisting both of organs for warmth and of organs for cold—only one of the two feelings can be experienced: if one is, the other ceases to be, and vice versa. But that the two feelings are nevertheless not opposed to each other is shown by the fact that if a warm stimulus and a cold stimulus are at the same time applied, respectively, to one of the cutaneous organs for warmth and to one of those for cold, both feelings are experienced together. The things that are mutually exclusive and lie on one scale of opposition instead of two are not the two feelings, but the physical temperatures that serve as stimuli to them respectively.

What perhaps leads Collingwood to believe that there is opposition of a sort other than opposition to a zero is the sort of situation we should have in a case where two things, each capable of existing in various degrees, happened to be distinct in the sense that no contradiction was involved in the supposition that either should exist or not exist, whether the other did or not; while at the same time, although each was opposed only to its own zero, the zero of each always in fact turned out to coexist with the maximum of the other (and analogously for the other degrees). No examples of two such things occur to me, and perhaps there are none; but even if any exist in philosophy or elsewhere, they do not illustrate a "fusion" of distinctness and opposition, nor a new sense of either of these terms.

11. *Three Easy Confusions Accounting for the Surface Plausibility of Collingwood's Methodological Precepts.*—Many other of Collingwood's contentions are equally questionable, but those already criticized are the ones on which his theories of the nature of philosophy and of the processes and structure distinctive of philosophical thought essentially depend, and with which they stand or fall. So likewise with the methodological precepts he lays down for philosophers. We may therefore here rest the case against all these, and conclude with a brief account of the reasons for such prima facie plausibility as the precepts themselves may have in spite of their unsoundness. Three easy confusions adequately account for it.

The first has to do with the kind of value philosophy essentially seeks to have. Collingwood, rightly, never doubts that the imposing systems constructed in the past by the great philosophers are achievements of high human value. What he seems to neglect, however, is that what these philosophers were striving to reach was knowledge, properly so called, concerning the matters they considered; that they very largely failed in this; and that the high value their constructions nevertheless have had is of a kind other than that peculiar to knowledge. As already pointed out, the value they have had has been chiefly as articles for possibly helpful faiths, or as more or less fanciful pictures representing beautiful or reasonable worlds that could serve as pleasant imaginative escapes from facts too often tragically stupid. This is to say that philosophy, in spite of the failure, in such large part, of its own search for knowledge, has been a good deal of a success in terms of the demands of persons who took it as nonrevealed religion or as poetic literature about man and the cosmos. And, for success of this sort, a "literary" as contrasted with a precise use of words is not only permissible but of great aid; while any errors or confusions that may result from it hinder little or not at all.

Collingwood's belief that traditional philosophy has been what philosophy ought to be, and his injunction upon the philosopher to make a literary and not a technical use of words, mean that the theory of philosophy which consciously or unconsciously he actually is defending, is that philosophy is essentially poetic literature about the world and man's relation to it, and therefore that philosophy is good when it has the characteristics which would make literature of this kind good.

This brings us to the second of the confusions referred to above. The eulogistic connotation of the word "literary" evidently compels us to reject any suggestion that philosophy should use words in an unliterary manner. This makes the assertion that it should use them in a literary manner plausible without regard to its ambiguity. But if by that assertion is meant that in the search for philosophical truth we should use words in the manner appropriate to "literary" purposes, then the assertion ceases to be plausible as soon as we realize that literary purposes are such things as aesthetic enjoyment, imaginative stimulation, expression and communication of feelings, moods, and attitudes. For although these purposes are quite as worthy as any, they are yet quite other than the purpose of discovering truth. What the latter requires is a use of words which, instead of being literary in the sense just indicated, is on the contrary "rational" in the sense that it makes dependable reasonings possible. And this means a use of words which is consistent, unambiguous, and precise even when this requires it to become technical. Just that is what constitutes a literary use of words in such writing as philosophical and scientific literature, which essentially aims to be not poetic, dramatic, imaginative, or biographical, but heuristic.

With this we come, third, to technical terms. Whenever, in any field, knowledge beyond what is common begins to be won, the introduction of technical terms quickly becomes indispensable; for a technical term, far from being, as Collingwood asserts, an arbitrary innovation in vocabulary created by verbal definition, on the contrary represents, in highly compressed form, genuine knowledge previously won, or a definite hypothesis about to be tested. Therefore, as Whewell has abundantly shown, technical terms are the products of, or the programs for, always "real" and never merely "verbal" definitions. For merely verbal definitions are bi-verbal definitions, and create not a technical terminology, but only a jargon—a new, esoteric language into which, for the convenience of condensation, it is sometimes desirable to translate portions of the old, the mere translation, however, constituting no addition to knowledge. A technical term, on the contrary, aims to express an addition to knowledge, i.e., to be the name of something real: of a theory that has been or can be verified, of a distinction corresponding to a difference that exists, etc.

Collingwood's assertion that in philosophy we only come to know better what we already to some extent knew before is true only in the sense in which it is also true that in theoretical physics we only come to know better the nature, already to some extent known to us, of the material objects around us. Such a situation, then, is in no way peculiar to philosophy. Rather, it is of the very essence of analysis, no matter what the subject. That it does not relieve us of the need of technical terms is evident enough in the case of physics. The reason why it does not relieve us of that need is that analysis, although indeed only making us know better what we in a way already knew, is often itself possible only in terms of entities (whether physical or other), which, although they were implicit all along in what we already knew, are nevertheless completely novel to us, and therefore call for novel names exactly as do newly discovered chemical elements or prehistoric animals.

CHAPTER FOUR

Philosophy as Light on Social Problems

IN AN address before an audience of philosophers a few years ago,[1] Otto urged attention to the fact that today vast numbers of men and women are in complete bewilderment as to what, if anything, the many activities in which they find themselves so strenuously engaged are ultimately about. The beliefs upon which were based the old rules of the art of living, he points out, are no longer widely and deeply held; and no new conception of the meaning of life, which would give one a sense of the relative importance of things, has been offered by philosophers to replace the old ideology. Instead, philosophers busy themselves with minute epistemological problems or with grandiose conceptions of reality equally devoid of bearing on the questions that the times ask, and properly ask, of philosophy.

1. *The Present Need for a "Philosophy of Life."*—What philosophy should be, Otto believes, is "philosophy of life." Its proper task is to seek fresh visions of the meaning of life wherewith to replace those that are gone, and to translate the new insights it obtains into rules for the art of living.

---

[1] *Op. cit.*

Moreover, the philosopher cannot gain these new insights by working "in superior isolation from other thinkers," but rather by becoming "literally a colaborer with those whose contributions are relevant to the task, so that together they may devise a philosophy not of contemplation but of practice."

2. *The Instrumentalist Theory of Knowledge.*—The outstanding protagonist of this view of philosophy, of course, has been Dewey, from whom Otto quotes the admonition that philosophy should change from "a device for dealing with the problems of philosophers" to "a method, cultivated by philosophers, for dealing with the problems of men."[2]

Dewey's conception of philosophy, its task, and its method, has its bases on the one hand in the instrumentalist theory of knowledge, and on the other in a profound interest in social improvement. The instrumentalist theory of knowledge appeals in the first place to the biological fact that man is an animal living in an environment, and that his self-preservation depends not only on adapting himself to that environment, but still more, and typically, on his attacking it in such manner as to cause, in the phenomena occurring naturally in it, advantageous changes that would not occur apart from his interference.[3] Dewey puts it thus:

The organism acts in accordance with its own structure . . . . upon its surroundings. As a consequence the changes produced in the environment react upon the organism and its activities. The living creature undergoes, suffers, the consequences of its own behavior. This close connection between doing and suffering or undergoing forms what we call experience.[4]

---

[2] Dewey et al., *Creative Intelligence* (1917), p. 65.
[3] *Ibid.*, p. 9.
[4] *Reconstruction in Philosophy*, p. 86.

Experience in this sense is the condition of foresight; and "knowing is the act, stimulated by this foresight, of securing and averting consequences."[5] A knower, then, is not a spectator but an agent; knowledge is not passive, disinterested contemplation, but is essentially active and directive:

[It] is not something separate and self-sufficing, but is involved in the process by which life is sustained and evolved. The senses lose their place as gateways of knowing to take their rightful place as stimuli to action. To an animal an affection of the eye or ear is not an idle piece of information about something indifferently going on in the world. It is an invitation and inducement to act in a needed way. It is a clue in behavior, a directive factor in adaptation of life in its surroundings. It is urgent, not cognitive, in quality.[6]

Thus knowledge "*is always a matter of the use that is made of experienced natural events*, a use in which given things are treated as indications of what will be experienced under different conditions."[7] Knowing is "the directive presence of future possibilities in dealing with existent conditions"; it is "a way of employing empirical occurrences with respect to increasing power to direct the consequences which follow from things."[8] It is essentially for the sake of doing; it is an instrument—a directive instrument—for altering the environment in a beneficial manner.

Yet instrumentalism does not mean "the use of thought to accomplish purposes already given either in the mechanism of the body or in that of the existent state of society," for "action restricted to given and fixed ends . . . . is mechanical (or becomes so)." The pragmatic, or instrumentalist, theory of intelligence is on the contrary that

[5] *Cre. Int.*, p. 61.
[6] *Reconstr. Phil.*, p. 87.
[7] *Cre., Int.*, p. 47.
[8] *Ibid.*, pp. 53, 59.

Intelligence develops within the sphere of action for the sake of possibilities not yet given. . . . . Intelligence *as* intelligence is inherently forward-looking. . . . . A pragmatic intelligence is a creative intelligence, not a routine mechanic. . . . . Intelligence is . . . . instrumental *through* action to the determination of the qualities of future experience. But the very fact that the concern of intelligence is with the future, with the as-yet-unrealized . . . . makes the action in which it takes effect generous and liberal; free of spirit.[9]

3. *The Instrumentalist Conception of Philosophy and Its Method.* —Philosophy, however, "claims to be one form or mode of knowing," and what is true of knowing in general and of the method by which knowing in general is achieved must therefore be true also of philosophy itself and of the method for philosophical knowing. The method must be the empirical, functional, genetic method of the natural sciences, which deals with denoted existences, seeks functional relations between them, and throws conclusions open to verification by setting forth the existential situations in which the conclusions offered had their genesis.[10] When, as a result of insight into the essentially instrumental nature of knowledge, philosophy is "released from vain metaphysics and idle epistemology,"[11] it, too, becomes "not a contemplative survey of existence nor an analysis of what is past and done with, but an outlook upon future possibilities with reference to attaining the better and averting the worse." Philosophic thinking is

caught up in the actual course of events, having the office of guiding them towards a prosperous issue. . . . . Philosophy is vision, imagination, reflection . . . . and these functions, apart from action, modify nothing and hence resolve nothing. But in a complicated

---

[9] *Op. cit.*, p. 63 f.
[10] Dewey, *Experience and Nature*, chap. i.
[11] *Reconstr. in Phil.*, p. 124.

and perverse world, action which is not informed with vision, imagination, and reflection, is more likely to increase confusion and conflict than to straighten things out.

Philosophy thus "recovers itself when it ceases to be a device for dealing with the problems of philosophers and becomes a method, cultivated by philosophers, for dealing with the problems of men."[12]

If we ask what problems Dewey means by the latter, the answer is that they are social and moral problems. Philosophy should

face the great social and moral defects and troubles from which humanity suffers . . . . concentrate its attention upon clearing up the causes and exact nature of these evils and upon developing a clear idea of better social possibilities; in short, upon projecting an idea or ideal which, instead of expressing the notion of another world or some far-away unrealizable goal, would be used as a method of understanding and rectifying specific social ills.

4. *Does Philosophy Consist of Prospective Thinking in General?*— Now, there can be no doubt of the need of fundamental improvement in social institutions and relations, nor of the fact that vision, imagination, reflection (and, one may add, humane feeling) are of the first importance in "defining difficulties and suggesting methods for dealing with them."[13] But it is far from evident that either the exercise of these faculties in general, or their employment specifically in the task of diagnosing and prescribing for social ills, is what constitutes philosophy.

Let us consider each of these two suppositions. Dewey at one point draws a contrast, which elsewhere he does not usually stress, between knowledge and thinking, science and philosophy. It is of assistance, he says,

---

[12] *Cre. Int.*, p. 65.
[13] *Democracy and Education*, p. 381.

to connect philosophy with thinking in its distinction from knowledge. Knowledge, grounded knowledge, is science; it represents objects which have been settled, ordered, disposed of rationally. Thinking, on the other hand, is prospective in reference. . . . . Philosophy is thinking what the known demands of us—what responsive attitude it exacts. Hence it is hypothetical, like all thinking. . . . . Its value lies not in furnishing solutions (which can be achieved only in action) but in defining difficulties and suggesting methods for dealing with them.[14]

As to this I would remark that "thinking what the known demands of us," i.e., making hypotheses, is an intrinsic part, not indeed of already acquired knowledge, but of all knowing, of the acquiring of knowledge, no matter of what. The chemist, physicist, physiologist, etc., in their attempts to explain the known, are every day called upon to perform that prospective, forward-looking activity; but they do not in the least *eo ipso* become philosophers. On the other hand, knowledge on a question admittedly philosophical, e.g., knowledge that metaphysics is vain and epistemology idle— which, if Dewey's arguments are valid, is then "grounded knowledge"—would none the less on that account be philosophy; although *after* it is attained it would of course no longer be philosophi*zing*. The fact is, then, that "thinking," i.e., the making of hypotheses, and the vision, imagination, and reflection it involves, are intrinsic elements of the process of acquiring new knowledge equally about such nonphilosophical questions as that of the origin of cosmic rays or the validity of Fermat's last theorem, and about such philosophical questions as whether it is true (as Dewey asserts) that "no theory of Reality in general, *überhaupt*, is possible or needed,"[15] or whether the instrumentalist account of the

14 *Loc. cit.*
15 *Cre. Int.*, p. 55.

nature of experience is correct. Prospective thinking thus has no special connection with philosophy or philosophizing, and therefore cannot possibly be regarded as differentiating philosophy from other forms of knowledge or knowing.

5. *Does Philosophy Consist of Prospective Thinking Specifically to the End of Social Improvement?*—On the other hand, the application of prospective thinking—the exercise of vision, imagination, reflection—specifically to the task of diagnosing social ills and formulating possible solutions for them is not any more than the preceding instance describable as philosophy. For what truly corresponds to the employment of these faculties specifically to such ends is not philosophy in general; indeed, it would hardly even be social ethics or social philosophy in general, but rather socio-ethical casuistics.[16]

Indeed, that, in spite of unqualified statements such as some of those already quoted, it is not really the nature of philosophy and philosophizing that Dewey is attempting to describe, but rather the nature of a worthy task which he believes persons trained in philosophy could perform well, is suggested by a number of his own statements. His account of the nature of recovery in philosophy, for instance, is introduced as a "conception of the present scope and office of philosophy";[17] and towards the end of the same section he writes:

I believe that philosophy in America will be lost between chewing a historic cud long since reduced to woody fiber, or an apologetics for lost causes (lost to natural science), or a scholastic, schematic

---

[16] I use "casuistics" rather than the more orthodox term "casuistry," because the latter has acquired a derogatory connotation, and I wish to avoid any suggestion that the employment I refer to is in any way to be looked down upon. On the contrary, I regard it as of great importance. But this is no reason for applying to it a description, viz. "philosophy," which belongs to something else.

[17] *Ibid.*, p. 53.

formalism, unless it can somehow bring to consciousness America's own needs and its own implicit principle of successful action. This need and principle . . . . is necessity of a deliberate control of policies by the method of intelligence.

This, however, is virtually to say that what comes before in that essay, or at a number of other places in Dewey's writings, in relation to philosophy, is not really a characterization of the species of knowledge called philosophical, or of the species of thinking called philosophizing, but is rather the description of a task now important in America which persons who in some (as it now appears) unstated sense are "philosophers," and more specifically American philosophers, would be well-fitted to perform.

6. *Knowing Originally but Not Essentially a Guide to Adaptive Behavior*.—Some remarks on the relations of knowledge to the lives of men will furnish a useful perspective on the instrumentalist account of knowledge and on the inferences that instrumentalism draws as to the nature, the method, and the functions of philosophy.

That knowledge is capable of serving as guide to action performed towards the preservation or improvement of life was long ago emphasized by Schopenhauer, who, it will be recalled, somewhere describes the intellect as a light which the will-to-live kindles for its own use. It may well be granted that the emergence, i.e., the origin, of imagination, thought, and knowledge—and indeed most of their development also—must be traced to their enormous utility as guides to prosperous action. But Schopenhauer perceived and emphasized also the fact that, in man at least, knowledge and sensation do on countless occasions become for the time emancipated from the service of action, whether adaptive of self to environment or of environment to self. It is precisely at such times that man discovers himself to be different in kind and not only in degree from the other animals. The latter for the most part relapse into sleep when their faculties are not being exercised in the service of their needs; but man lives most truly as man only in the free exercise of his faculties, which begins when his needs are satisfied, or indeed sometimes even before they are satisfied. Whenever a man's attention is wholly absorbed by a beautiful color, a sweet odor, a delicious taste, or the like, the assertion that sensation is "an inducement to act in a needed way . . . . a clue in behavior" patently fails to describe what sensation is then to him. For in every such case sensation is on the contrary something self-sufficing, something free from the service of adaptive behavior.

For man, thought also—imagination, reflection, cognition —can and often does become divorced from behavior-guiding function. It is then a form of activity engaged in for its own sake, in complete freedom from preoccupation as to any utility either biological or social that it may or may not have. It is at just such times that man truly emerges from the animal level; for when he exercises his intelligence to plan and direct the construction of even a Hoover Dam or an Empire State Building, he is after all only an educated and exceptionally intelligent beaver. Thought distinctively human is typified much rather by the case of the astronomer who, absorbed in the study of the stars, forgets at the moment that his mind lives in an animal, and falls into a well; or by the case of the poet who, as the "intelligent beaver" sees it, hasn't sense enough to use his faculties to make a living, and starves in his garret.

It is just because the intelligence of man is thus not essentially or always "planning thought," because his reason does not by its very nature have to be "used in the creation of social arts," and does not necessarily have "something to do,"[18] but is on the contrary capable of genuine freedom from the task of "increasing power to direct the consequences which follow from things," that Dewey's contrast between the "problems of philosophers" and the "problems of men" is question-begging and wholly inadmissible. For philosophers too are men, and even the most abstract or technical of the problems of philosophers are some of the problems of men. Thinking and knowing, whether they be for man efficient or inefficient means to living, are, for the intellectually developed man, themselves in considerable measure self-justifying modes of living. They have, that is to say, a greater or less measure of intrinsic value to him, not only in addition to any functional value they may have, but in spite of at times total lack of functional value, or even in spite of functional disvalue. How far at a given time a man can afford to think solely for the joy of thinking is of course a matter of how far the fruits of his own earlier utilitarian thinking have won for him freedom from the practical need. But whatever the amount of such freedom possessed by a man, the instrumental relationship of thought to life gives way for him to its converse in the measure to which thinking no longer depends on the goad of need: for him, in that very measure, life is for thought, not thought for life.

Moreover, such "esthetic consecration"—to use Santayana's phrase—of an activity which originally had only functional value is not here an evil as it is when that which has become loved for itself is a special instrument rendered by changed circumstances now harmful instead of useful. On the contrary, the free exercise of thought—the exercise of inventiveness, curiosity, imagination, reflection, not because of any pressure of need but just because they itch for

---

[18] *Reconstr. in Phil.*, p. 96.

exercise—is a good both because man finds in it one of his keenest satisfactions, and because its very freedom from preoccupations with social betterment makes possible discoveries that often turn out to have most important applications for social betterment, but which never would have been made had such betterment been the aim.

Such reflections move one to wonder whether a certain easy confusion is not perhaps at the basis of the instrumentalist contention that knowing or inquiry is essentially a means or guide to adaptive behavior—the confusion, namely, of the truth that thinking of the inquisitive sort is essentially a means to problem-solving, with the error that the problems to be solved themselves always concern the means to an end. The fact is that some do and some do not. If the problem I seek to solve is "How could I remove this spot from my coat," thinking or inquiry is a means to discovery of the solution, i.e., it is a means to discovery of the means of removing the spot. In this case the problem does concern the means to an end. On the other hand, if the problem I seek to solve is "How many satellites has Jupiter," thinking or inquiry is again a means to discovery of the solution; but in this case the problem to the solution of which thinking is a means is not itself a problem as to means. In my own case at least, there is no ulterior end for the sake of which I seek as means a knowledge of the number of these satellites. My curiosity as to their number is disinterested, free. It is idle, not working, curiosity. It has doubtless a cause, but no purpose. And cases of such free curiosity are innumerable not only among scientists but also among laymen. The discovery of fossilized dinosaur eggs or of a new outlying planet, for instance, is so interesting to the general public—although it can do nothing with it—that the discovery is front-page news.

7. The Instrumentalist Conception of Freedom in Thinking.— It may be said, however, that the instrumentalist himself distinguishes between free and "servile" thought, and therefore that the facts above instanced must be compatible with the instrumentalist view. But I shall now attempt to show that the manner in which he proposes to distinguish between free and servile thought simply does not work and therefore does not reconcile the instrumentalist account of thought and knowledge with those facts.

A passage earlier quoted makes clear that Dewey regards thought as servile when it is "a mere means for an end already given," even if the end "is labeled moral, religious, or aesthetic"; i.e., it is servile when it is employed to direct the accomplishment of "purposes already given either in the mechanism of the body or in that of the existent state of society." An example of servile thought thus would be, we may assume, thought devoted by a man to increasing the yield of the farm which is the means to the satisfaction of his hunger and to other ends which, like the satisfaction of hunger, are ends "given in the mechanism of the body." Another example would be, presumably, thinking devoted to increasing the efficiency of means for transportation or long-distance communication, or for other such "purposes already given. . . . in the mechanism . . . . of the existent state of society."

On the other hand, thought is free according to Dewey when it is used "to project new and more complex ends"; when it is engaged in planning "action for the sake of possibilities not yet given . . . . action directed to ends to which the agent has not previously been attached."[19] Examples of free thought would then presumably be the imagining and planning of some new form of government, the defining of some new theory of education, etc.

---
[19] *Cre. Int.*, pp. 63 f.

Let us see, now, whether the distinction proposed will serve. An example of the employment of thought in planning "action directed to ends to which the agent has not previously been attached" would clearly seem to be the thought used in the invention of the airplane, for flying was a "possibility not yet given" to man, and for the sake of which the inventor's creative thought and action were being employed. Such thought was therefore free according to the definition proposed. But that inventor's same creative thought and action could just as truly be described as having been devoted to the devising of a more efficient means to a purpose "already given . . . . in the mechanism . . . . of the existent state of society," viz., the purpose of transportation. That inventor's same thought must therefore be also described as servile. The distinction proposed between free and servile thought thus will not work.

Again, government, education, etc., are ends already given from ancient times by the mechanism of society. The devising of new forms of government or education would then be a devising of more efficient means to already given ends; and such devising would according to the distinction proposed then be a servile employment of thought. But that very same employment of thought is also free according to the distinction proposed; for if we describe what it attempts to devise by a specific name—e.g., fascism, communism, or the project method in education—instead of in terms of its relation to government or education in general, then what is being devised is automatically also describable as "possibilities not yet given . . . . ends to which the agent has not previously been attached." The distinction proposed between free and servile thought thus has no objective basis.

The truth of the matter would seem to be that all thinking which is not simply repetitious and merely habitual (i.e., not any longer properly thinking at all, since often a machine can better accomplish the same tasks) is genuinely creative, and this quite irrespective of whether what it creates is the conception of a new means to an end already given, or the conception of a new end to which to turn means already available. Thus, the distinction between ends already given and ends not yet given has nothing to do with the creative, forward-looking character which belongs to all genuine thinking. And therefore that distinction has nothing to do with the difference between free and servile thinking, which it purported to define. The two kinds of thinking are equally creative, heuristic.

The true distinction between free and servile thinking is, I submit, that between thinking because one likes to, and thinking because one needs to. And since the two are not necessarily exclusive, the test in any given case is: Would the thinking be carried on even if one knew that what it creates or discovers can be of no possible use in guiding action to the improvement of life for one's self or others? If it would not then be carried on, it is essentially servile, or, as I should prefer to phrase it, essentially in the service of needed control over the conditions of life, even if the performance of the thinking also happens to be enjoyed. If on the other hand the mere satisfaction of curiosity, the mere intellectual adventure of exploring possibilities, the mere joy of creating or inventing, would be sufficient to motivate the thinking, then it is essentially free, even if one also happens to hope that the knowledge it achieves will turn out to be of some use in directing action for social betterment.

From Dewey's conception, which would identify philosophy with thought devoted to social improvement, let us now turn to Bertrand Russell's, which would identify it with logic.

CHAPTER FIVE

Philosophy as Identical with Logic

During the last hundred years the science of logic has made vastly more progress than it did in all the centuries since its foundation by Aristotle; and today a growing number of mathematicians and philosophers are actively carrying the subject forward. The appearance of Whitehead and Russell's *Principia Mathematica* in 1910 was one of the outstanding events in the history of its modern development, and among philosophers the question was soon asked what bearings the logical achievements it typified might have upon philosophy. A few years later Russell attempted to answer this question by formulating the conception of the nature of philosophy and of scientific method in philosophy to which he found himself led.[1] It is to the view of the nature and method of philosophy then described by him that we now turn.

1. *Russell's Definition of Philosophy.*—"Philosophy," Russell declares, "is the science of the possible."[2] This statement is intended by him to sum up two distinctive characteristics of

---

[1] Bertrand Russell, *Our Knowledge of the External World* (1914); *Mysticism and Logic and Other Essays* (1919), chap. vi.

[2] *Myst. Log.*, p. 111.

any philosophical proposition, viz., it must be general, and it must be a priori.

To say that a philosophical proposition must be general means that "it must not deal specially with things on the surface of the earth, or with the solar system, or with any other portion of space and time. . . . . A philosophical proposition must be applicable to everything that exists or may exist."[3] Moreover, the view that philosophy is general in this sense is sharply different from the view that it is general in the sense that its propositions have "the universe" or "the whole" as their subject. Russell maintains on the contrary "that there are no propositions of which the 'universe' is the subject; in other words, that there is no such thing as the 'universe'."[4]

The propositions of philosophy are general, he holds, in the sense that they "may be asserted of each individual thing, such as the propositions of logic," i.e., they formulate "properties which belong to each separate thing, not . . . . properties belonging to the whole of things collectively";[5] and these properties are to be those that belong not only to each separate thing that exists, but to each that may exist.

By saying, on the other hand, that a philosophical proposition must also be a priori, Russell means that it "must be such as can be neither proved nor disproved by empirical evidence." Philosophy "must make only such assertions as would be equally true however the actual world were constituted."[6]

2. *Philosophy Indistinguishable from Logic.*—But to say that generality and apriority, in the senses defined, constitute the

---

[3] *Op. cit.*, p. 110.
[4] *Loc. cit.*
[5] *Ibid.*, pp. 110 f.
[6] *Ibid.*, p. 111.

distinctive characteristics of philosophical propositions, is to say that philosophy "becomes indistinguishable from logic as that word has now come to be used."[7] Logic, however, consists of two parts. One is the study of "those general statements which can be made concerning everything without mentioning any one thing or predicate or relation, such for example as: 'If x is a member of the class a and every member of a is a member of β, then x is a member of the class β, whatever x, a, and β may be."[8] This part "merges into pure mathematics, whose propositions all turn out, on analysis, to be such general formal truths."[9]

The other part of logic "is concerned with the analysis and enumeration of logical *forms*, i.e., with the kinds of propositions that may occur, with the various types of facts, and with the classification of the constituents of facts. In this way logic provides an inventory of possibilities, a repertory of abstractly tenable hypotheses."[10] This second part is philosophically the more important. It "investigates what propositions are and what forms they may have . . . . enumerates the different kinds of atomic propositions, of molecular propositions, of general propositions, and so on."[11]

What Russell regards as included in this second part of logic —and therefore of philosophy—is made clearer by reference to the meaning he assigns to some of the terms used in his description of that part. By a proposition, for instance, he means "a form of words which must be either true or false."[12] By a fact, he means "that a certain thing has a certain quality, or that certain things have a certain relation."[13] By an

---

[7] *Loc. cit.*
[8] *Ibid.*, p. 112.
[9] *Our Kn. Ext. World*, p. 57.
[10] *Myst. Log.*, p. 112.
[11] *Our Kn. Ext. World*, p. 57.
[12] *Ibid.*, p. 52.
[13] *Ibid.*, p. 51.

atomic proposition, he means one "which expresses . . . .
a fact"; by a molecular proposition, one which contains a
conjunction, e.g., *if, or, and, unless*; by a positive general
proposition, one containing the word *all*, e.g., "all men are
mortal"; and by a negative general proposition, one containing the word *some*, e.g., "some men are philosophers."[14]

Since philosophy is declared by Russell to be "indistinguishable from logic" as he conceives the latter, the
problems of philosophy, according to the passages cited, are
then (1) to discover those "supremely general propositions,
which assert the truth of all propositions of certain forms,"[15]
and (2) to analyze and enumerate possible logical forms.
Thus "every philosophical problem, when it is subjected
to the necessary analysis and purification, is found either
to be not really philosophical at all, or else to be, in the
sense in which we are using the word, logical."[16]

3. *Traditional Metaphysics Not Knowledge, but Only Wishful
Thinking.*—As indicated by Russell's assertion, above quoted,
that there is no such thing as the universe and therefore that
no proposition has the universe as subject, metaphysics in
the traditional sense of the term is according to him not
possible. He considers the building of cosmological systems
as no more possible than the discovering of the philosopher's
stone, and thinks that philosophy can do nothing whatever
to satisfy our hope that the world has this or that desirable
ethical character.[17] The systems that have claimed to do this
represent, he believes, not knowledge but only the products
of wishful thinking. The philosophy that seeks knowledge

---

[14] *Op. cit.*, pp. 52 ff.
[15] *Ibid.*, p. 57.
[16] *Ibid.*, p. 33.
[17] *Ibid.*, p. 26.

in a sense of this term as strict as the sense it has when applied to the results of the sciences "must deal with somewhat dry and abstract matters, and must not hope to find an answer to the practical problems of life. . . . . Many hopes which inspired philosophers in the past it cannot claim to fulfil; but other hopes, more purely intellectual, it can satisfy more fully than former ages could have deemed possible for human minds."[18]

Unwelcome or even mistaken as this view of metaphysics may be, it is obviously not disposed of by Hoernlé's objection that the method Russell advocates for philosophy imposes upon it a complete reorientation, a new task altogether, and is therefore an instrument for doing well something other than the traditional tasks of philosophy, not a better instrument for doing these.[19] A medieval alchemist might similarly have argued, and with similar irrelevance, that the methods of modern chemistry (had they been described to him) are not better instruments for achieving the traditional tasks of alchemy—the distilling of the elixir of life, etc.—but only impose upon alchemy a complete reorientation, a new task altogether!

4. *Philosophical Method Essentially Analytical.*—Philosophy, Russell declares, "does not become scientific by making use of the other sciences. . . . . Philosophy is a study apart . . . . its results cannot be established by the other sciences, and conversely must not be such as some other science might conceivably contradict."[20] For success in philosophizing, a certain mental discipline is the first requisite. The desire to know philosophical truth must not be obscured by the desire

---

[18] *Ibid.*, pp. 29 f.
[19] *Stud. Con. Met.*, p. 42.
[20] *Our Kn. Ext. World*, pp. 236 f.

to think we know such truth. It must be strong enough to survive failure after failure to gain the desired knowledge; and it must not be obscured by love of system, or by desire to establish this or that agreeable result. Again, methodological doubt must be practiced in order to loosen the hold of mental habits; and logical imagination must be cultivated to acquire fertility in imagining abstract hypotheses.[21]

When this mental discipline has been acquired, the method of philosophical investigation is found to be essentially analytical. Philosophical problems, as they present themselves, are usually complex and must be analyzed into their component problems. This usually reveals "that a number of . . . . extraordinarily abstract questions underlie any one of the big obvious problems." Eventually a stage is reached where progress requires "some new effort of logical imagination, some glimpse of a possibility never conceived before"; and if this is successful, then "from this point onward, the work of the philosopher is synthetic and comparatively easy."[22]

To illustrate this general description of the process of philosophical discovery, the problem of space as presented in Kant's "Transcendental Aesthetic" may be considered. Russell states that analysis soon shows three distinct problems to be involved. One of them is logical, and is that of the nature of geometrical reasoning; another is physical, namely, that of finding or constructing a physical space having the logical properties of some one of the kinds of space geometry defines; and the third, which is epistemological, is that of showing how synthetic knowledge a priori of space is possible. Of the first, a complete solution is possible, and of the second a solution which is approximate, as are the solutions

---

[21] *Op. cit.*, 237 ff.
[22] *Ibid.*, pp. 241 f.

of other problems in empirical regions. The solution of these two problems has the result of showing that the assumption on which the third is based, viz., that synthetic knowledge a priori of space is possible, is, if not certainly false, at least devoid of the plausibility it had prior to the analysis.[23]

5. *Russell's Account of the Nature of Philosophy Incompatible with His Examples.*—The tasks of logic, it will be recalled, are described by Russell as, on the one hand, to discover "certain supremely general propositions, which assert the truth of all propositions of certain forms"; and, on the other hand, to investigate what propositions are and to make an inventory of the possible forms of propositions. Since he declares that when logic means this, philosophy is indistinguishable from logic, these tasks must then also be the tasks of philosophy.

I submit, however, that Russell's account of the process of philosophical discovery, summarized in the preceding section, is an account of the manner of performance of a task other than these; and, further, that both the analytical investigation of the problems of space or of the external world, which Russell offers as illustrations, and likewise the bulk of his other philosophical (vs. purely logical) writings, are examples of attempts to perform tasks other than those of philosophy as he defined them. For to break up some obvious big philosophical problem into its constituent problems—e.g., the problem of space as stated by Kant into a logical, a physical, and an epistemological problem—and to solve the logical and the physical problems, is something quite different from making an inventory of the possible forms of propositions or of facts, or from classifying the possible constituents of facts, or from discovering supremely general propositions.

[23] *Myst. Log.*, pp. 114-20.

To have performed these latter logical tasks puts one in possession of a logical apparatus which may well be of the greatest help, or even indispensable, for the solution of philosophical problems. But the fact remains that to seek such logical apparatus, i.e., to labor at the discovery or at the perfection of it, is one task; whereas to utilize this apparatus, i.e., to labor by means of it at the solution of problems other than logical (such as those of judgment, perception, etc.) is quite another task. The first is the task of logic; but the second is the task of any science—for instance of philosophy or of physics—for the solution of whose problems a more or less technical logical apparatus needs to be employed. Any science, that is to say, is in some measure applied logic. The subject matter of logic does consist of propositions completely general and a priori. But this is not the case with the subject matter either of philosophy or of any natural science, however much any progress in them may be dependent on possession of an adequate logical equipment. The subject matter of any science other than logic (which includes mathematics) is both specific and empirical.

The point of these remarks may be further emphasized by considering such a presumably philosophical work as Russell's *Analysis of Mind*. This work is not devoted to the question: Which forms of propositions, or types of facts, are possible, and which propositions are supremely general? It is, on the contrary, an attempt to decide whether certain propositions about introspection, belief, truth and falsehood, perception, etc., are certainly or probably true. To decide this, it is no doubt of great help to discern clearly which form, of all those that propositions may have, the propositions considered about these things do have. But even to attempt to discern this is not to labor at a theory of propositions or at an inventory of possible propositional forms. To attempt to decide whether the propositions considered, of which we may have succeeded in discerning the form, are true or false is to labor at still another task, also different from that which Russell describes as the task of logic and of philosophy.

6. *Russell's Account of the Nature of Philosophy Unsound.*— But we are then faced with the following choice: either such a work as *The Analysis of Mind* is not a philosophical work, or else (since it is not a work on logic) philosophy is something distinguishable from logic. I take it that few will have any hesitation in deciding that this work is philosophical, and that philosophy, whether or not it includes logic as a part of itself, is something distinguishable from logic. Russell himself, indeed, at more than one point writes in a way implying the existence of a distinction between philosophy and logic. For instance, he says about the study of logic that "it *gives the method of research* in philosophy, just as mathematics gives the method in physics" (italics mine).[24] This implies that the study of logic and the study of philosophy are just as distinguishable as in fact are the study of mathematics and the study of physics, even granted that in each case the first is necessary to the second, and that attempts to solve the problems of the second may stimulate us to develop the first.

But if logic is, as giver of method or as instrument, related to philosophy as mathematics is to physics, the conclusion which Russell there draws—viz., that "the study of logic becomes the central study in philosophy"—certainly does not follow. What does follow, if the alleged parallelism of relation is a fact, is that logic is the central study, not in philosophy, but as equipment for research in philosophy.

---

[24] *Our Kn. Ext. World*, p. 239.

7. *Differentiation of Philosophy from Logic No Reflection on the Value of the Analytical Method.*—The employability of the analytical method in philosophy is not dependent on the assumption that philosophy is indistinguishable from logic, and the falsity of that assumption therefore has no bearing on the value this method may have there. Whatever conclusion we may eventually reach as to what philosophy essentially is, the employment of the analytical method in it as elsewhere makes for clearness and definiteness; and these are qualities much to be desired in philosophy, since it is in large measure the failure to achieve them that has rendered philosophical investigation so frequently barren. Russell's own use of the analytical method furnishes many convincing examples of its power to bring to light the issues fundamental in various philosophical problems and to define them sharply. Thus, although analysis can hardly be described either as a distinctively philosophical method, or as the whole of the method of philosophy, there can be no doubt that there is in philosophy abundant occasion for employment of it.

CHAPTER SIX

Philosophy as Systematic Study of Meanings

THAT philosophy is the systematic study of meanings, and comprises all the rational sciences, is the thesis argued by S. K. Langer in a book published some years ago.[1] She traces the origin of this conception of philosophy to Socrates, who constantly professed to be inquiring into the meaning of such concepts as justice, knowledge, etc. But Socrates' practice, Langer finds, did not actually conform to his program. He was "a sophist, not a scholar"; persuasion was his aim, whether he realized it or not; and the course of his would-be analyses of concepts was surreptitiously affected throughout by the predetermined conclusions that were to be reached. The program, however, was sound, and "had Socrates taken his own advice and followed the meaning of even a single term, such as 'good,' or 'soul,' or 'happiness' through its confused and intricate connotations to something like clarity of definition, he would have founded the philosophical sciences."[2]

1. *Philosophy as Comprising All the Rational Sciences.*—However, the very sort of program which Socrates set himself is

---

[1] *Op. cit.*
[2] *Ibid.*, p. 24.

that of certain sciences, of which logic and mathematics are the best known, viz., the rational sciences: "they never did and never will have recourse to observation and experiment . . . . they are not in pursuit of *facts*, but of *meanings*. They are not empirical, but rational sciences."[3] Not only logic and mathematics, however, but also metaphysics, theology, theory of value, theory of knowledge, and ethics are—or, by availing themselves of the logical technique today available, can become—truly rational sciences, "systems produced by developing the implications of a few fundamental ideas";[4] and therefore the proper method of metaphysics, like that of logic and mathematics, is a close attention to *implications*."[5] Philosophy, then, comprises "all the rational sciences"; it is "a group of disciplines which are all governed by the principle of seeking . . . . *logical connections*, just as the other great group, natural science, is governed by the principle of seeking *causal connections*."[6]

Among the rational sciences, metaphysics is the one which "makes explicit all that a concept such as, for instance, 'the World' or 'Life' contains; it seeks to discover the *meaning*, first of 'unity,' 'time,' 'causality,' etc., and ultimately of such terms as 'Reality,' 'Truth,' 'Infinity,' and 'God.' "[7] Among the rational sciences, metaphysics "has the same sort of priority . . . . as physics among the natural sciences."

2. *The Place of Analysis and Construction in Philosophy.*— "Logical analysis is to philosophy just what observation is to science—namely, the first step in finding and formulating a

---

[3] *Op. cit.*, p. 31.
[4] *Ibid.*, p. 33.
[5] *Ibid.*, p. 35.
[6] *Ibid.*, p. 36.
[7] *Ibid.*, p. 35.

problem, and a means of testing the answer."[8] But analysis is not the only nor even the chief method of philosophy. Analysis has done its work when it has led us to a genuine paradox, for then *"we have found the point where our real problem arises."*[9] But "the greater part of philosophy . . . . is the construction of concepts which shall fulfil all the uses of those [to which analysis has led us] which were logically untenable, and avoid all their abuses."[10] The task is then "to find a new and acceptable *meaning* for the word whose denotation we recognize, but whose definition was absurd. This is the point where creative ability, ingenuity, original-ity, in fact all the powers of philosophical genius come into play."[11]

3. *Philosophy and the Natural Sciences.*—When the nature of philosophy, as described above, is understood, "it is easy to see . . . . why the sciences not only are, but must be, born of philosophy."[12] Every science "is built upon definite *basic concepts*"; but "the definition and systematization of general fundamental notions belong to philosophy, and the precise determination of them is the philosophical labor which scientists must either do, or accept from others, before their science can stand on its feet."[13] Thus it is that "a natural science is philosophical until, and only until, it is scientifically respectable," i.e., until it reaches the point where "it shows signs of being true, of explaining phenom-ena." But "none of its *philosophical* propositions will ever be replaced by *scientific* ones."[14]

---

[8] *Ibid.*, p. 37.
[9] *Ibid.*, p. 67.
[10] *Loc. cit.*
[11] *Loc. cit.*
[12] *Ibid.*, p. 41.
[13] *Ibid.*, p. 40.
[14] *Ibid.*, pp. 39, 41.

4. Definition and Systematization of Fundamental Concepts a Late Stage in the Development of a Natural Science.—Langer's statement of her conception of the nature of philosophy, now outlined, is clearer and more definite than most, and when it is considered in connection with some of the writings of philosopher-logicians such as Russell or Whitehead, it has a certain plausibility. That conception seems to me, however, to be quite untenable for a number of reasons that I shall now attempt to state.

We may begin with the conception of the relation between philosophy and natural science and the explanation, as above summarized, which it offers for the historical lack of clear distinction between philosophy and infant natural science. Is it, I ask, historically true that the initial stages of a natural science are intrinsically philosophical in the sense of consisting of definition and systematization of the basic concepts of the science? I submit that what the history of the natural sciences on the contrary seems to show is that the definition and systematization of the fundamental notions of a science are a late stage in its development. Not only is this allegedly philosophic labor not a temporal prerequisite for enabling science to stand on its feet and to discover true laws and explanations of phenomena, but it is even a labor which in fact cannot be performed or profitably attempted until the science has, on its own power as natural science, both got on its feet and traveled a long way.

Physical science, for example, really owes the concepts of the atom and the molecule, and the definition of them, not to Leucippus, Democritus, or Epicurus, but to the need it had of these concepts as means of explanation and prediction of certain facts which became known only at a rather advanced stage of its development. There can be no doubt that physical science would have introduced and defined them

at about the time it did, and as it did, even if the atomistic
cosmology of these philosophers had been unknown to Dal-
ton, Avogadro, Gay-Lussac, or the other physical scientists
of the period. As Dampier points out, "exact quantitative
measurements of the proportions in which chemical elements
combined by weight and by volume . . . . led irresistibly to
the idea of atoms and molecules." The Greek theory, not
being founded on definite experimental facts, nor tested by
its consequences in experience predicted on the basis of it,
"remained a doctrine, like the metaphysical systems in
ancient and modern times, dependent on the mental attitude
of its originators and their followers, and liable to be upset
and replaced from the very foundations by a new system of a
rival philosopher. And this indeed is what happened."[15]

5. *Investigation of the Meaning of Concepts Not the Differentia
of the Rational Sciences.*—Let us now turn to another and
much more decisive objection to the view that philosophy,
or rational science, consists in the systematic study of meanings. That the rational sciences do inquire into the meaning
of certain concepts is true enough, but the contention that
they are the only sciences that do so, and that this constitutes
their differentia, is startling indeed in view of the fact that
examples are numberless to show that the natural sciences
also do just this, although the concepts in question are not
the same. To mention but a few, such concepts as salt, acid,
gas, liquid, solid, water, air, iron, etc., are concepts the exact
meaning of which is investigated and discovered not by
metaphysicians, logicians, or mathematicians, but by chemists and physicists; and the same is true of such even more
basic physical concepts as light, electricity, matter, mass,

---

[15] Sir William Dampier, *A History of Science* (1936), p. 24.

etc. Moreover, although physicists and chemists do give us precise accounts of the meaning of these and numerous other concepts, they do so in their capacity as natural scientists, i.e., on the basis, ultimately, of observations and experiments, and not merely of reflective "attention to implications," as is the case with the investigations of meaning carried on within the field of logic and mathematics.

So far as the meaning of concepts goes, what distinguishes the rational from the natural sciences is not that the former do and the latter do not investigate this—for both do—but much rather what kinds of concepts each attempts to define. Since Langer overlooks this, she of course does not attempt to state the difference between the two kinds of concepts; nor does she, so far as I can find, attempt to say what differentiates the concepts investigated by metaphysics from those investigated by the other rational sciences. She indicates what they are only by means of a few examples such as reality, truth, infinity, God. But the very kernel of the problem is to discover and describe accurately what the characters are that differentiate concepts such perhaps as these, which are "metaphysical," from those which are logical, or mathematical, or natural-scientific. Instances of metaphysical concepts, even if admitted to be such, are only the material for the induction to be performed, and do not tell us what we want to know, namely, what its outcome would be if it were performed.

As we shall see later, the search for definitions and the attempt at systematization, far from being the differentia of the rational sciences, are features of any science, whether natural, rational, or philosophical, in proportion as it becomes advanced and theoretical.[16] That even a natural science, in so far as perfected, seeks to order its propositions

---

[16] Cf. M. Cohen, *Reason and Nature* (1931), pp. 106–114.

in the form of a deductive system does not, however, make of it even in part a "rational science," if that term means any science which takes possible forms of deduction as its subject matter. On the other hand, even the rational sciences, which investigate possible forms of deduction and of combination, etc., do, in proportion as they are not far advanced, present their propositions about this as discoveries that are more or less isolated and independent or, as we may say, "logically empirical," rather than—as increasingly later— in the form of a deductive system in which all such propositions are exhibited as implications of a few postulates and rules. Thus, arrangement of propositions in logically systematic form is one thing, and investigation of the nature of logically systematic form is another, and either can to a considerable extent go on without the other. Langer's identification of rational science with the investigation of meaning would seem to have no more solid basis than a failure to keep in mind the distinction between the two— between science which is rational in the sense of having a highly systematic logical form, and science which is rational in the sense of having the nature of systematic logical form as its subject matter.

In any case, the bare fact that the natural sciences, as such, do investigate the meaning of numberless concepts stands immovably in the way of Langer's proposal to define rational science—to say nothing of philosophy—as the systematic study of meanings. And it stands in the way even in face of the distinction she stresses between logical connections and causal connections, even, that is to say, if it should be true that the concepts whose meaning is investigated by natural science are to be defined ultimately in terms of conjunctions of causal properties, and those whose meaning is explored by rational science, in terms of logical properties. For Langer's contention was that rational science (including philosophy) is the systematic study of meanings, not just of one category of meanings.

It might be said, of course, that what natural science investigates is not, for instance, the concept "acid," but the things called acids. Yet there is a concept "acid," and chemistry, not philosophy, does tell us its exact meaning. That concept, however, is of empirical origin, and to analyze its meaning is therefore not possible simply by reflective "attention to implications." Because it is an empirical concept, whatever definition of it may suggest itself will have to be a "real," not an arbitrary, "nominal" definition. That is, the definition will have to represent either a direct induction from certain observations, under experimental conditions, of things called acids, or else a hypothesis about things called acids (no matter how it suggested itself), susceptible of being disproved or given support by observation of the things called acids under certain experimental conditions. If a definition of "acid" represents neither of these, it can only represent a piece of psychological testimony by the person who advances it, viz., testimony as to the properties which the word "acid" happens to call up in his own mind.

The fact is that a descriptive concept either is created outright by stipulation of what one proposes to mean by a word —and in this case the meaning is explicit to begin with—or else the concept arises as a spontaneous result of attention to a variety of things that have certain characters in common. In this case the concept is always more or less obscure (although generally adequate to many practical purposes) and requires analysis before use can be made of it for theoretical purposes. But in the case of such concepts it is important to note that to investigate their meaning is one and the same thing as investigating the set of respects in which the things denoted resemble one another and differ from all others. That is, in such cases, the intension of the word, the meaning of the concept, and the essential nature of the things to which the word is applied, are exactly the same thing; and to investigate one is to perform precisely the same operation as to investigate either of the others.

6. *Broad's Failure to Give the Differentia of Concepts that Philosophy Alone Investigates.*—C. D. Broad, whose conception of philosophy Langer's closely resembles in some respects, is not much more explicit as to the differentia of philosophical concepts. Philosophy, or at least critical as distinguished from speculative philosophy, is defined by Broad as "the analysis and definition of our fundamental concepts, and the clear statement and resolute criticism of our fundamental beliefs";[17] and this of course immediately raises the question: Which ones among our concepts are to be described as "fundamental?" Broad illustrates them by mention of the concepts of thing, place, date, change, cause, substance, etc. He also says that the special sciences (as well as common sense) use these concepts, but that "it is not their business to enter, more than is necessary for their own special purposes, into the meaning and relations of these concepts as such."[18] This, of course, does not define the term "fundamental"; but Broad seems even to give away the very essence of the contention that analysis of meaning of "fundamental" concepts is the differentiating task of (critical) philosophy when he adds:

Of course the special sciences do in some measure clear up the meaning of the concepts that they use. . . . . But the special sciences only discuss the meanings of their concepts so far as this is needful for their own special purposes. Such discussion is incidental to them,

---

[17] *Scientific Thought* (1923), p. 18.
[18] *Ibid.*, p. 16.

whilst it is of the essence of philosophy, which deals with such questions for their own sake.[19]

This not only leaves unanswered the central question, viz., what specific character marks a concept as "fundamental," but deprives us of the possibility of answering it even only negatively and obviously too narrowly by saying, as seemed suggested, that they are the concepts which the special sciences use but do not need to investigate. For to tell us that it is not their business to investigate the meaning of such concepts as mentioned "more than is necessary for their own special purposes" is to tell us that it *is* their business just so far as it is their business. I submit that in so far as it is not their business, the concept is not fundamental specifically to them; i.e., such parts or aspects of the meaning as it is not their business to investigate are in no way fundamental but on the contrary irrelevant *to them*. These very parts or aspects would however be fundamental to a task quite other than the tasks of these sciences, viz., to that of discovering what a science in general, or perhaps a physical science in general, is. Such a task, obviously, is philosophical. But to recognize this still is not to answer the question as to what exactly differentiates this and other admittedly philosophical tasks from tasks that are not philosophical.

7. *Different Nature of the Premises for the Assertions of the Rational Sciences vs. those of Philosophy.*—Another decisive objection to Langer's conception of philosophy is that there is a certain character which belongs to pure mathematics and pure logic, but which philosophy has never claimed but rather always repudiated. This character is that the facts by appeal to which pure mathematics and pure logic prove or disprove the propositions they assert always in ultimate analysis consist of stipulations, viz., of postulates, rules, and

---

[19] *Ibid.*, pp. 16 f.

biverbal definitions. This means that what these sciences do is essentially to develop the implications of certain conventions; and no matter what reasons of psychological convenience or of practical interest may exist for making one rather than another convention, such conventions, from the standpoint of pure logic and mathematics, are wholly arbitrary. Another way of stating the same fundamental fact is by saying, as Russell does, that pure mathematics and logic constitute the science of the possible. One may put the fact still otherwise by saying that, within pure logic or mathematics, the question never arises whether any real thing exists that has the properties in terms of which logical and mathematical concepts are defined. For these sciences are not trying to describe what exists, but only what is logically possible.

But obviously the case is radically different with philosophy. The propositions it formulates are not advanced as implications of arbitrary conventions respecting the meaning that shall be attached to certain terms or symbols. They are advanced as propositions which are either certainly or probably true about knowledge, or about truth, or reality, or beauty, or goodness, or whatever their subject may be.[20] If it be said that what philosophy attempts is to analyze the meaning of these terms, this may be admitted, provided that the definitions in which that meaning is eventually stated are not merely "verbal" definitions or implications of verbal definitions or defining postulates, but on the contrary "real" definitions. This means that they must be statements of the nature of something which was not created (whether explicitly or implicitly) by means of a stipulation as to the meaning of some terms, but existed independently of such creative conventions. To say that it existed independently of them means that at least the part of the thing's nature that

---

[20] Broad, *op. cit.*, pp. 19 f.

we seek to discover is logically independent of the manner in which the thing was presented to our attention, and is therefore not discoverable deductively by "attention to the implications" of that manner. For example, if some one asks "What is this tree?" it is not an answer to his question to say: "It is a physical, space-occupying, vegetable object, having branches, roots, bark," etc. For this is to answer another question which he did not ask, and to which he presumably already knows the answer well enough for his purposes, viz., the question, "What is a tree?" His question concerns the characters of "this" which are neither logically deducible from the concept "tree" nor immediately obvious to him in the mere perceiving of the object about which he asks his question, e.g., the character of being an oak, or of being deciduous, etc.

To illustrate the radical defect that inevitably attaches to any philosophy which offers itself as a science of the same kind as pure logic and mathematics, no better example can be found than Spinoza's system. For even if the chains of implications he attempts to develop should all be as rigorous as he intended to make them, the final and philosophically crucial question would remain whether his basic definitions and axioms (i.e., postulates) are arbitrary and merely conventional like those of pure mathematics and logic, stipulating what he proposes to mean as for instance by the word "substance," or on the contrary represent statements somehow already discovered to be true about some existing thing, which thing, previous to that discovery, the word only denoted but did not describe. For if Spinoza's definitions and axioms do not represent statements of the latter sort, then all that he builds upon them by attention to their implications constitutes nothing but one out of many logically possible alternative castles, or rather universes, in the air. It only constitutes an elaboration of what is implied by certain arbitrary statements initially made, and of what would be true if these initial statements should not merely have been made but should happen in addition to have a real and not merely verbal subject, and to be true of that subject. Thus, there is a radical incompatibility between, on the one hand, the claim which Spinoza, in common with practically all other philosophers, tacitly makes, that the propositions embodying his philosophy are not merely mutually consistent and some deducible from others, but have as subject the world (or parts of the world) in which we empirically find ourselves, and are true of that world; and, on the other hand, the claim (whether made by him or for him) that his system is or attempts to be "rational" in the sense of purely formal, like pure logic and mathematics, which deals not at all with an empirical world as such, but only with logically possible forms of worlds or of anything else.

The theoretical constructions of philosophy cannot be arbitrary in the sense in which a postulate-set can be arbitrary when it does not attempt to be such that deduction from it of certain propositions specified in advance shall be possible. This means that philosophy is not a rational science in any but the elliptical sense in which one could so describe theoretical physics (because it makes use of mathematics), as distinguished from the mathematics considered in itself that theoretical physics uses, which on the contrary is a rational science in the literal sense of the term. For whereas mathematics needs only to be free from contradictions, physics, no matter how theoretical and mathematical it may be, seeks always to be true of the world in which we empirically find ourselves and is thus fundamentally a natural and not a rational science.

CHAPTER SEVEN

Philosophy as Logical Syntax of the Language of Science

CONSPICUOUS among recent attempts to differentiate philosophy from other intellectual enterprises is the one made by the logical positivists. Carnap, who is perhaps at present the most prominent member of the "Vienna circle," in particular has contended that philosophy is the logical syntax of the language of science. It is this contention that we must now examine.

1. *What Carnap Says Philosophy Is Not.*—Reduced to their most summary form, Carnap's contentions concerning the nature of philosophy are as follows:

The traditional problems of philosophy may be classified under three heads: logical, psychological, and "metaphysical." Metaphysical propositions Carnap defines as "all those propositions which claim to represent knowledge about something which is over or beyond all experience."[1] But no proposition is even theoretically verifiable unless from it are deducible propositions of perception, different if it were true from what they would be if it were false. Propositions metaphysical in the sense of over or beyond all experience are

---

[1] *Philosophy and Logical Syntax* (1935).

therefore essentially unverifiable. But a proposition which is not even theoretically verifiable is, speaking logically as distinguished from psychologically, without sense—meaningless.[2] Propositions that are metaphysical in the latter sense, and therefore nonsense, include, Carnap asserts, not only the propositions of what has traditionally been called metaphysics, but also those of traditional epistemology and of normative ethics. They are really pseudo-propositions; that is, they seem to express a judgment or assertion, but in fact express only a command or an emotional attitude. Psychological propositions, on the other hand, are not meaningless, since they are empirically verifiable; but to say that they are so verifiable is to say that they belong to empirical science, not to philosophy. This leaves for philosophy only problems of logical analysis.[3]

I am here concerned only with the thesis that philosophy is logical syntax and I shall therefore not pause to examine Carnap's dismissal of metaphysics. I may say in passing, however, that although his use of the term metaphysics seems to me unfortunate, I hold that a statement is ambiguous for us if we can not specify any respect in which our experience (whether perceptual or other) would, under specified circumstances, be different if the statement were false and if it were true. It seems to me, moreover, that many of the statements found in books on metaphysics, epistemology, and other parts of philosophy, are of precisely this kind; that is, we do not know of any test of them which, if applied, would either prove them, or disprove them, or show them either less or more probable than their alternatives. Therefore, for the purposes of anyone seeking knowledge, such statements are wholly negligible. And this, I believe, is substantially what

---

[2] *The Unity of Science* (1934), p. 26.
[3] *P. L. S.*, pp. 9–34; also, *The Logical Syntax of Language* (1937), pp. 277–81.

Carnap means when he describes them as "nonsense" or "meaningless."

2. *Philosophy as Logical Analysis, i.e., Syntax of the Language of Science.*—But what is logical analysis? It is the sort of investigation of which the results are expressed in syntactical sentences—in sentences of logical syntax.[4] A syntactical sentence is a sentence expressing either a formation rule or a transformation rule of a language system (or a consequence of such rules), that is, either a rule for determining how kinds of expressions to be called sentences of that system can be constructed out of the different kinds of symbols or words (e.g., nouns, articles, adjectives, verbs, etc.) or a rule for determining how given sentences may be transformed into others.[5] Whether a given word is, e.g., a noun, or a verb, etc., is then a matter not of what it stands for but either of the rules for combining it with others or of the form of the word itself.[6] Syntactical sentences thus concern only the *form* of a language; that is, they do not concern the sense of any sentence of that language or the meaning of any of the words entering into its sentences, but only the arrangements of its words, and the derivation of sentences of it one from another. Using the word "formal" in this sense, the logical syntax of a language may therefore be defined as "the *formal* theory of that language."[7]

By the language of *science*, Carnap means "the use of language for making assertions," viz., the part of language consisting of declarative sentences as distinguished from questions, commands, exclamations, etc.[8] Therefore when he

---

[4] *P. L. S.*, p. 68.
[5] *Ibid.*, pp. 41, 43.
[6] *L. S. L.*, p. 2.
[7] *P. L. S.*, p. 39.
[8] *Foundations of Logic and Mathematics*, International Encyclopedia of Unified Science, I, No. 3, p. 3.

defines philosophy as the logical syntax of the language of science, he means that philosophy is concerned exclusively with the rules of formation and transformation of declarative sentences (and the consequences of those rules), wholly without regard to what the words which make up the sentences stand for.

3. *Ambiguity of the Term Syntax as Used by Carnap.*—However, the reader who is attempting to discover what exactly he is to understand by the word syntax is much handicapped by the fact that Carnap uses it in three or perhaps even four more or less different senses:

1) In some places, he refers to syntax as being investigation —specifically, analytical investigation, viz., analysis: "The logical syntax of a language system S consists of . . . . the investigation or analysis of the formation rules of S, and that of the transformation rules of S.[9] Similarly, by implication, when, having defined language as "the *system of the rules* of speaking," he refers to languages as "objects of logical syntax,"[10] that is, presumably, objects of the kind of investigation called logical syntax. Again, in such an expression as "the task of syntax is . . . ."[11] syntax is apparently being conceived as an enterprise, viz., an investigative one.

2) Elsewhere, Carnap uses "logical syntax" as the name of a theory, "a theory which we will call Logical Syntax";[12] that is, apparently, as the name of a *particular sort of theory* (in the way in which we might refer, e.g., to the corpuscular

[9] *P. L. S.*, p. 45. See also *L. S. L.*, p. 315, where the logical analysis of physics is stated to be "the syntax of the physical language." See also *F. L. M.*, p. 1, where the logical analysis of language is presented as consisting of semantics and syntax.
[10] *P. L. S.*, p. 41.
[11] *Ibid.*, p. 58.
[12] *Ibid.*, p. 39.

as distinguished from the wave theory of light). But he also and more deliberately and often refers to logical syntax as the theory *of a particular sort of subject*, viz., of the formal aspects of language: "the formal theory of language (known as 'syntax' in our terminology)";[13] "the formal theory of the linguistic forms of . . . . language."[14] Such theory, i.e., logical syntax, is then more particularly described as consisting of the system of formation and transformation rules of a language: "we apply the name 'syntax' . . . . to the system containing [not formation rules only but] both kinds of rules together."[15]

But as pointed out above, a system of such rules is elsewhere called by him *a language* and languages are called *objects* of logical syntax. Elsewhere, a language is stated to be a calculus, and a calculus itself stated to be a system of rules of formation and transformation; and logical syntax is then described as "the construction and manipulation of a calculus."[16]

3) On still other occasions, Carnap speaks of "the syntactical method,"[17] syntax then apparently being conceived neither as language nor as theory nor as investigation, but as a method of investigation.

4. *Syntactical Sentences and the Formal Mode of Speech.*—This erratic employment of the word syntax is puzzling indeed to the reader, who finds the word or its adjective used on practically every page. However, for the purpose of grasping and assaying the contention that philosophy is logical syntax,

---

[13] *L. S. L.*, p. xvi.
[14] *Ibid.*, p. 1.
[15] *P. L. S.*, p. 47; *L. S. L.*, p. 2.
[16] *Ibid.*, pp. 4, 5.
[17] *P. L. S.*, pp. 39, 68; *L. S. L.*, p. 8, "the method of syntax," and p. 11, "the syntactical method."

it need perhaps be remembered only that a "syntactical sentence," in any case, is a sentence formulating either a formation or transformation rule of a language or a consequence of such rules, and that, according to Carnap, if a sentence is neither metaphysical (and therefore devoid of sense), nor psychological, and yet is philosophical, it is then always really a syntactical sentence. Sentences obviously syntactical are said to be in the "formal mode of speech," the mode, namely, which we use in so far as we speak exclusively of words or other symbols and of the rules for constructing sentences out of them and transforming these sentences into others.[18]

The contention that all genuine philosophical sentences are really syntactical is based by Carnap on a distinction between what he calls "real-object" sentences, "pseudo-object" sentences, and syntactical sentences. He holds that all philosophical sentences which have sense but do not present themselves as syntactical are of the pseudo-object kind; that every sentence of this kind can be translated into a syntactical sentence; and that every pseudo-object sentence is thus shown to concern not a real object but only a linguistic form. Let us first be clear as to the kinds of sentences Carnap designates by those names.

5. *Real-Object Sentences.*—Real-object sentences are "sentences which concern not linguistic expressions but extralinguistic objects,"[19] stating, for example, properties or relations of such objects.[20] Or, more technically, real-object sentences are "synthetic" sentences: "*synthetic sentences are the genuine statements about reality.*"[21] A synthetic sentence

[18] *P. L. S.*, p. 64.
[19] *Ibid.*, p. 60.
[20] *L. S. L.*, p. 277.
[21] *Ibid.*, p. 41.

is itself defined as a sentence which is both not analytic (i.e., is not a consequence of every sentence) and not contradictory (i.e., is not such that every sentence is a consequence of it). A synthetic sentence, in other words, is one which is a consequence of only certain sentences, and of which only certain sentences are consequences.[22]

6. *Pseudo-Object Sentences and the Material Mode of Speech.*— A pseudo-object sentence, on the other hand, is one which *seems* to concern objects because there are used in it words designating objects or matter, but which really concerns linguistic forms.[23] More explicitly, pseudo-object sentences "are formulated as though they refer (either partially or exclusively) to objects, while in reality they refer to syntactical forms, and, specifically, to the forms of the designations of those objects with which they appear to deal."[24] From this it follows that in reality "it is only possible, in any domain of science, to speak either *in* or *about* the sentences of this domain, and thus only object-sentences and syntactical sentences can be stated."[25] Pseudo-object sentences, which are said by Carnap to be in the "material mode of speech," are accordingly described by him as "quasi-syntactical sentences of the material mode of speech."[26]

7. *"Translation" of Sentences of the Material Mode of Speech into the Formal Mode.*—The majority of philosophical sentences, Carnap points out, present themselves in the material mode of speech; and, as already mentioned, his ground for asserting that in spite of their appearing thus to concern

---

[22] *Ibid.*, pp. 39, 40.
[23] *P. L. S.*, pp. 60, 64.
[24] *L. S. L.*, p. 285.
[25] *Ibid.*, p. 331.
[26] *Ibid.*, p. 285.

objects, they nevertheless really concern linguistic forms and therefore really are disguised syntactical sentences, is that (he believes) all sentences of the material mode of speech can be translated into the formal mode. This translatability, indeed, is declared by him to be "*the touchstone for all philosophical sentences,* or, more generally, for all sentences which [have sense but] do not belong to the language of any one of the empirical sciences."[27]

The process he designates as "translation" from the one into the other mode of speech turns on the existence of syntactical qualities that are "parallel" to qualities of real objects in the following sense: "a syntactical quality Q_2 is called *parallel* to the quality Q_1 [of an object] if it is the case that when, and only when, an object possesses the quality Q_1 does a designation of that object possess the quality Q_2."[28] On the basis of this definition, the criterion of a pseudo-object sentence (at least when those of the simplest form are concerned) is this: "such a sentence attributes to an object (say a) a quality Q_1 to which a parallel syntactical quality Q_2 can be found. Such a sentence 'Q_1 (a)' can then be translated into the syntactical sentence 'Q_2 ('a')' which attributes the quality Q_2 to a designation of that object."[29]

8. *"Translatability" from the Material into the Formal Mode No Proof that Philosophy is Syntax.*—Before turning to the question whether the process called by Carnap translation from the material into the formal mode of speech is really translation, it is worth noting that even if it really were translation, his conclusion that sentences in the material mode really are disguised syntactical sentences, and therefore that philosophy is really syntax, would not follow. What

[27] *Op. cit.*, p. 313.
[28] *P. L. S.*, p. 63; also, *L. S. L.*, p. 287.
[29] *P. L. S.*, p. 63.

would follow would be that *either* they are disguised syntactical sentences, *or* the syntactical sentences into which they
are translatable are disguised sentences of the material mode,
i.e., are really sentences about objects (and if so, their truth-
value can be ascertained by observation of objects). For if a
sentence S is truly and exactly a translation of a sentence Z,
then Z is equally truly and exactly a translation of S. And
therefore one could assert that such translations into the
formal mode are in truth pseudo-syntactical sentences—i.e.,
are quasi-objective sentences of the formal mode. One could
assert it on the very same ground and the only ground—viz.,
translatability—offered by Carnap for asserting that philosophical sentences are in truth pseudo-object sentences and
are to be described as quasi-syntactical sentences of the
material mode.

It would thus be perfectly arbitrary which one of such a
pair of sentences we chose to describe as a "disguise" of the
other, and which one therefore to describe as what the other
"really" is; and therefore it would be arbitrary also whether
we chose to say that philosophy is really syntax or that
syntax, or at least a certain part of syntax, is really philosophy. This point, which in itself has perhaps no great
importance, is good at least to show that, even on Carnap's
own premise of translatability, his numerous statements that
syntactical sentences are the "correct" way of stating what
sentences of the material mode "really" are, and that the
latter are but "disguises" of the former, represent nothing
that he has in the least demonstrated, and are thus wholly
dogmatic. But I believe and shall now try to show that even
the alleged translatability is not a fact.

9. *What Carnap Calls Translation into the Formal Mode of
Speech Not Truly Translation.*—An example offered by Carnap
of a sentence in the material mode of speech—or a pseudo-

object sentence—is, "This book treats of Africa"; and the syntactical sentence which he offers as "translation" of it into the formal mode is, "This book contains the word Africa" (or an expression synonymous with this word).[30]

Common sense, however, distinguishes between a sentence and the fact, opinion, or hypothesis which the sentence formulates; and when in ordinary English one sentence is said to be a translation of another, what is meant is that both sentences formulate exactly the same fact, opinion, or hypothesis. An example would be the two sentences "This book treats of Africa" and "Ce livre traite de l'Afrique." But I submit that the two sentences "This book treats of Africa" and "This book contains the word Africa" do not formulate the same fact but each a different fact, and therefore that the second is not a translation of the first at all. For the continent called Africa is one thing and the word Africa is another, wholly distinct; and no statement of the relations the word Africa has to certain other words can possibly be a translation, properly so called, of—that is, be strictly synonymous with —any statement about something, such as the piece of land called Africa, which is other than a word.

It may be possible, it is true, to give a rule for matching certain statements about the piece of land called Africa each with a statement about the word Africa having the same truth-value. There would then be a parallelism of truth-values between the statements of the two sets, and perhaps even between statements derivable from those of each set. But parallelism of truth-values, even if systematic, is one thing, and synonymy is another; for in spite of the parallelism of truth-values, the statements of the two sets would remain formulations of facts or opinions in the one case about a

---

[30] *Op. cit.*, pp. 61, 65.

word, and in the other about a piece of land, and thus cannot be translations of each other.

That the sentence "This book contains the word Africa" is not a translation of the sentence "This book treats of Africa" would in any case be proved by the fact that the truth-value of each is independent of that of the other. For there can be a book that contains the word Africa and yet is not about Africa—for instance, a rhyming dictionary, or a book describing Australia but miscalling it Africa. And there can be a book about Africa which does not contain either the word Africa or an expression synonymous with it. An example would be a book consisting of the following sentence: "The continent about which I am writing contains forests in which gorillas live." For the expression, "the continent about which I am writing," is not in English synonymous with the word Africa. It obviously does not have the same connotation; and as regards denotation, whereas the word Africa does orient the attention of English-speaking readers or hearers to a specific region of the earth's surface, the expression given does not do this even if the author's name appears on the book and much less if the book happens to be anonymous. Indeed, even if the expression were instead "this continent," I should have to insist that it would not be synonymous with the word Africa; for what identifies for another person the continent concerned is not the words "this continent" by themselves (as on the contrary the word Africa by itself does identify it), but perception by the other person both of the pointing gesture performed at the time by the utterer of those words, and of the presence of a continent at the place pointed to.

Before passing to other examples of "translation" offered by Carnap, let us examine what he claims to be the difference between the so-called pseudo-object sentence "This book treats of Africa" and the real-object sentence "Mr. A. visited Africa." He states that "it is really a quality of Africa to be visited by Mr. A.," but that "it is not a quality of Africa to be treated of in that book, because one might know everything about Africa and nevertheless nothing about that book."[31]

Obviously, however, the assertion that one might know everything about Africa and yet not know, about Africa, that it is treated of in that book, is a contradiction unless being treated of in that book is not a quality of Africa. Carnap's "evidence" that it is not a quality of Africa thus begs the very question at issue. What he needs to show, he merely asserts.

One can only guess at the criterion he employs to distinguish what is and what is not a quality of Africa. Being visited, i.e., presumably at least walked on, by Mr. A. is counted by Carnap as a quality of Africa. Would then being circumnavigated or being flown over, but never landed on, by Mr. A. be also counted as a quality of Africa? And on the other hand, if being treated of in a certain book is not a quality of Africa, then being treated of in the particular manner called being misrepresented would not be a quality of it either. But would Carnap be willing to say similarly that one could know everything about, for instance, the late Captain Alfred Dreyfus, without knowing that he was misrepresented as a traitor in certain documents? I submit that unless one knows this, one does not know one of the most outstanding facts about him. Likewise, unless one knows that certain Spaniards believed that a golden city or a fountain of youth existed in America, one does not know everything about

---

[31] *Op. cit.*, p. 65; see also *L. S. L.*, pp. 285–86, where Carnap uses "property" instead of "quality."

America, for even certain physical facts about America, viz., that certain Spaniards explored it, can be correctly explained only by reference to the fact that America was thought of by them as containing such things.

Carnap's contention that "This book treats of Africa" is "really" a statement of the relation of the word Africa to certain other words, has already been shown to rest only on his misdescribing as "translation" a process which is other than translation. The remarks just made show that his corresponding assertion—that being treated of in a certain book is not a quality of Africa—is supported only through a *petitio principii*; and that, beside being thus wholly dogmatic, it is on its own merits hardly plausible.

Let us now examine another of the examples Carnap gives of what he calls translation from the material into the formal mode of speech. He takes the sentence "The rose is a thing," and offers as translation of it into the formal mode the sentence "The word 'rose' is a thing-word."[32] The reason he gives for classifying the sentence "The rose is a thing" as a pseudo-object sentence, and for asserting that the other is a translation of it into the formal mode, is that the truth of the sentence "The rose is a thing" can be ascertained "without observing any rose, by only considering to what syntactical kind the word 'rose' belongs, namely that it is a thing-word."[33]

But, we must now ask, how can one tell whether or not a given word of the English language is a thing-word? The answer that would naturally suggest itself would be that it is a thing-word if that to which we choose to apply it is a thing—as distinguished from, for example, a property, or a place, or a relation, etc. But this does not seem to be what

---

[32] *P. L. S.*, pp. 61–62; *L. S. L.*, pp. 293, 297.
[33] *P. L. S.*, p. 62; *L. S. L.*, p. 293.

Carnap would answer. I believe he would say, rather, that a word is a thing-word if it is one which, according to the rules of formation of the language, can be combined only in certain manners M_1, M_2, etc., with certain other words W_1, W_2, etc.— perhaps, for instance, the word milk, in the following manners with the given other words: fresh milk, good milk, cold milk, etc.; drink milk, fetch milk, use milk, etc., etc.[34] For only an answer of this type would constitute a syntactical definition of thing-word.

The question would then arise, however, whether a word which is a thing-word as so defined is also a thing-word in the sense of being a word which is the name of a thing (as distinguished from a property, a relation, etc.). It seems that Carnap would decide this question in the affirmative by stipulation, that is, by ruling that whatever one chooses to designate by a given word is a thing if the word is a thing-word in the syntactical sense of this term; for he gives the rule, for example, that any two objects are to be "assigned to the same genus if their designations belong to the same syntactical genus"[35]

The proposal embodied in this rule, however, seems to make the extraordinary assumption that conventions (either made by us or already existing) as to word combinations create real likenesses between, or other real characters in, any real entities to which one may choose to apply the words entering into the conventions. But the plain fact, I submit, is on the contrary that the real characters of real entities are what determine the syntactical relations of the words by which we have chosen to designate the entities; and therefore that when we assert about such a real entity as a given rose

---

[34] Cf. Bloomfield, *Linguistic Aspects of Science*, Int. Enc. Unif. Sci., I, No. 4, p. 26, from which this example is borrowed, and to which Carnap refers his readers elsewhere (*F. L. M.*, p. 5).
[35] *L. S. L.*, p. 293.

(or inductively about any entity which is a rose), that it is a
thing, our assertion of this is based on the fact that observation of the given entity (or of any other entity which is a
rose) has revealed to us that, on the one hand, it resembles
such other real entities as trees, houses, mountains, stones,
etc.; and that, on the other hand, it differs from such other
real entities as solubility, combustibility, fusibility, malle-
ability, etc. (which we label not things but properties), and
differs also from such other real entities as "later than,"
"between," "two inches from," "helper of," "together
with," etc. (which we label not things but relations).[36]

If the "rules" for the combining of given particular words
such as rose and thing are not thus dictated by, and because
of this, parallel to, the real relations empirically discovered
as holding between the real entities we have chosen to label
by those words, then the laying down of formation rules is
just a verbal game with which we please to amuse ourselves;
and any parallelism there may turn out to be between such
rules and the relations of any entities that are real in the sense
of being other than words is then a pure matter of luck. But
obviously, the language to which the everyday words thing
and rose belong was not constructed in this arbitrary way;
nor were the words thing and rose retained in it because the
syntactical relations that had been assigned to them luckily
turned out to parallel the real relations of certain real entities
nor, still more strangely, because these words magically con-
ferred on any entities to which we chose to apply them real
relations parallel to those syntactical ones.

---

[36] In referring to such properties and relations as real, I do not mean anything more
or less metaphysical than does Carnap when he refers to, e.g., a rose, as a real object—
viz., that it is other than verbal. Since Carnap regards the questions debated in the controversy over universals as pseudo-questions (*ibid.*, p. 311), I assume that he would not
embrace the nominalism which would, as he does, class, e.g., a rose, as real, but would
refuse to call likewise real the properties or relations it has.

But if, as obviously is the fact in the case of the word thing, the syntactical rules for the combining of it with others are dictated by the empirically observed relations between the real entities to which we have tacked this and the other words, then these "syntactical rules," as well as the more particular sentences from which they are then generalizations, are in truth sentences formulating relations between real entities; and these sentences, if presented in the formal mode of speech, should then be described as quasi-objective sentences of the formal mode of speech.

The upshot of these remarks is then that when we assert of a given real entity that it is a thing, we do so because we observe it to possess a certain set of real (but determinable) characters; and that when we further assert of the same entity that it is a rose, we do so likewise because we observe it to possess a certain additional set of real (and likewise determinable) characters. The set of characters labelled *thing*, however, happens to be a part of the set labelled *rose;* and therefore if we have already observed that a given entity possesses the set of characters labelled *rose*, we can show, merely by analysis of what we have already observed, i.e., without additional observation of the entity itself, that it possesses also the set of characters labelled *thing*. But that in such a case this can be shown analytically is no evidence whatever for the contention that the analysis by which it is shown is syntactical analysis, viz., analysis of the relation of the word rose to a class of words called thing-words. For the reasons already stated, I contend on the contrary that it is real analysis, viz., analysis of the relation which a certain set of real characters has to a certain other set of real characters.

I contend, further, that actually we know that the word rose is a thing-word not by discovery that this is a consequence of the syntactical rules of English, but by inference from jointly (*a*) the empirically discovered fact that the set of real characters we chose to label *thing* is a part of the set we chose to label *rose*—i.e., the fact that the rose is a thing —and (*b*) the fact that if it is true that the rose is a thing then it is necessarily true also that the word rose is a thing-word. Theoretically, it might have been through investigation of the syntax of English that we learned that the word rose is a thing-word. We should have learned it in this way if, for instance, we had come upon books written in English and, without being able to know what real entities any of the words in them stood for, we had found that the word rose was often coupled in them by "is" with the word "thing" but never with such words as "property," "relation," etc. But actually this is not the way we learned it.

However, had the sentence used as example been instead, "The word 'chiliagon' is a plane-figure word," the contention that its truth is known by syntactical analysis would have been sound, for the word chiliagon came into English not as a label for the set of characters common to certain perceived real entities, but as the result of a prescriptive verbal definition; and therefore if we should ever identify a perceived real figure as a chiliagon, we should be doing so on the basis of that verbal definition.

On the other hand, it is worth noting that in the case of the word "circle," which—unlike chiliagon—came into the language as the name for certain perceived shapes, we do identify perceived real figures as circles (e.g., the figure of a coin, of the full moon, etc.) on the basis of their perceived shape and not on the basis of the geometer's prescriptive verbal definition of the word circle. Indeed, no figure we perceive can strictly be identified as a circle in the geometer's sense of the word.

To sum up now the argument of this section: Carnap contends: (*a*) that the truth of "the word rose is a thing-word" can be ascertained by only considering to what syntactical kind the word rose belongs; (*b*) that "the word rose is a thing-word" is a translation of "the rose is a thing"; and (*c*) that the truth of "the rose is a thing" can therefore be established without observing any rose, and merely by syntactical analysis.

As against this I have argued (*a*) that actually we know that the rose is a thing by empirical observation of the relation of the two sets of real characters we chose to label respectively *rose* and *thing;* (*b*) that actually we know that the word rose is a thing-word not through investigation of English syntax, but as an inference from our prior knowledge that the rose is a thing. And I now further urge (*c*) that although the truth of "the word rose is a thing-word" follows from the truth of "the rose is a thing," the first sentence concerns the relation of a word (viz., rose) to certain other words, whereas the second sentence concerns the relation of entities other than words (viz., real roses) to certain entities that are also other than words (viz., real things); and therefore that the two sentences do not formulate the same fact at all and cannot correctly be described one as translation of the other. Carnap would, I believe, grant that the discovery that a given entity is a flower is empirical and real and likewise the discovery that a given entity is a rose; and there seems no good reason why he should not grant also that discovery of the less specific fact that a given entity is a thing (and not perhaps a relation or a property) is likewise empirical and real. It is true that if the entity concerned is not given concretely, but only its name (e.g., "Caro") is given, then he can maintain, as he does, that if that name is not a thing-name, then (by the formation rules of the language) "Caro is a thing" is not to be called a sentence.[37] But this only brings up all over again essentially the same question we have discussed, viz., whether Caro is a thing-name as a matter of syntactical convention (whether already existing, or made by ourselves), or on the contrary in the sense that the real entity to which we choose to apply it is empirically observed by us to have a certain set of real characters, the set, namely, which we have previously chosen to label by the word thing.

Another allegedly pseudo-object sentence used as example by Carnap is, "The evening-star and the morning-star are identical." He gives as translation of it into the formal mode the sentence, "The words 'evening-star' and morning-star' are synonymous."[38] Carnap regards the first sentence as illustrating "the deceptive character of the material mode as to the subject matter of its sentences,"[39] since that sentence seems to assert a relation between two objects, although only one planet is concerned.

That sentence, however, actually illustrates only the fact that, in the material mode of speech as in the formal, it is possible to say only clumsily what one means; for the sentence can easily be freed of the defect mentioned and yet remain in the material mode. What it expresses only clumsily can be expressed accurately by "the star seen in the evening is identical with the star seen in the morning." This sentence formulates a belief really about a star observed in the morning and a star observed in the evening; and it resolves a possible doubt as to whether the star observed at the one time is or is not the same as the star observed at the other time. This

---

[37] *Op. cit.*, p. 293, ex. 1.

[38] *P. L. S.*, pp. 61, 66. In *L. S. L.*, p. 290, Carnap makes clear that by "synonymous" he means in this case "P-synonymous" and not "L-synonymous"—the difference between the two, stated in more familiar language, being roughly that between sameness of denotation and sameness of connotation.

[39] *P. L. S.*, p. 67.

sentence is thus not about the syntactical relation of one word to another at all, and the sentence, "The words evening star and morning star are synonymous," which formulates a syntactical relation, is therefore not a translation, properly so called, of it. What is true is only that there is a systematic parallelism of truth-value between two sentences so related; but although if a sentence is a translation of another such parallelism is present, the converse does not hold.

There is another example, viz., "This letter is about the son of Mr. Miller," which, although analogous to the one concerning Africa, is worth mentioning because Carnap there considers the possibility that Mr. Miller has no son. He states that even then one can deduce from this sentence, by the ordinary rules of logic, the sentence, "A son of Mr. Miller exists," which is nevertheless then false. And Carnap claims that this shows "that the use of the material mode of speech leads to contradictions if the methods of inference which are correct for other sentences are thoughtlessly used also in connection with it."[40]

But I submit that the example shows no such thing. It shows only that if one starts with a sentence which is false, then, whether it be of the material or of the formal mode, other false sentences can be logically deduced from it. Carnap, it is true, asserts that even if Mr. Miller has no son, the sentence, "This letter is about the son of Mr. Miller" may still be true (the letter "will then merely be telling a lie"!). But obviously this is not so. If Mr. Miller has no son, then (although the letter may still contain the expression "the son of Mr. Miller") what will be true of the letter will be, not that it is about the son of Mr. Miller, but only that it is about an imaginary son of Mr. Miller; and from this one cannot deduce that a son of Mr. Miller exists.

---

[40] *L. S. L.*, p. 291.

It is worth noting, moreover, that from the formal-mode sentence, "This letter contains a sentence in which occurs the description 'the son of Mr. Miller,' " one can logically deduce that "a letter exists containing a sentence in which . . . . etc." Yet this existential assertion may be false, for it may actually be false that this letter contains any sentence in which that description occurs, or indeed that any letter is there at all.

10. *"Psychologism" vs. "Chemistry of Symbols."*—Examination of additional examples would only confirm that what Carnap calls translation from the material into the formal mode is not really translation at all; and since the allegation that it is translation is the basis on which he rests the contention that philosophy is logical syntax, this contention collapses.

This, however, does not preclude the possibility that logical syntax is a part of philosophy. I do not now propose to go into its merits, but a word seems in order concerning what Carnap calls "psychologism," viz., the mistake, as he considers it, "that logic is a science concerning thinking, that is, either concerning the actual operation of thinking or the rules according to which thinking should proceed."[41] In this connection, he contrasts the "meaning" of a sentence in the sense of the thoughts, images, etc., connected with it, with its "meaning" in the sense of such other sentences as are consequences of the given sentence according to the transformation rules of the language to which it belongs. The latter alone is logical meaning or sense; the former, on the contrary, psychological.[42]

But to contrast logical with psychological meaning in this

---

[41] *P. L. S.*, p. 34.
[42] *L. S. L.*, p. 42.

manner seems to me indefensible for the following reason. The laws or rules of nature are properties which the entities of nature have quite independently of man's participation in the transformations that take place among these entities according to those laws. A stone dislodged from a cliff by the frost obeys the law of gravitation wholly without need of man's co-operation. But the laws or rules of formation and of transformation of a language are not similarly properties of its words and sentences themselves. Combinations of words into sentences, and transformations of the latter into other sentences in accordance with such rules, do not occur independently of performance of the combinations or transformations by a human mind. The fact plainly is that the formation and transformation rules of a language are properties not of its words and sentences but of some human mind or minds. That is, they are habits that some mind already has or that it purposes to adopt at least for a time. Indeed, a verbal entity is truly a word or a sentence at all only in so far as the habits of some human mind connect it regularly either with some non-verbal experience or with certain other verbal entities in specific ways.[43]

The rules of a language, I submit, thus are what Professor Carnap denies that they are, viz., ways in which certain minds think or propose to think on certain occasions, and ways in which the thinking of certain minds should proceed on certain occasions if it is to succeed in what it aims at. To deny this would be to imply that words can be endowed by man with quasi-chemical properties of their own in accordance with which they then become capable of combining independently of his presence.

That a language is a system of habits of human beings is

[43] Cf. the writer's "Symbols, Signs, and Signals," *Journal of Symbolic Logic,* IV (1939), 41.

indeed stated by Carnap himself in a recent publication.[44] It is quite true, as he also states,[45] that one can abstract from the speaker and deal only with the expressions of the language and their relation to their *designata*, or even deal only with the expressions. But to abstract from the speaker or hearer can properly mean only to take him for granted throughout without mention; not, of course, to suppose that logical rules, which are habits in him, are properties of symbols independently of him. The possibility of abstraction from speakers or hearers thus does not render compatible the two assertions made by Carnap, viz., that the rules of logic are not rules of the thinking of certain human beings, and that language and therefore its rules are a system of habits of human beings.

11. *Syntactical Treatment of Philosophical Problems.*—The criticisms set forth in the preceding pages seem to me to dispose of Carnap's contention that the only genuine philosophical problems are problems of the syntax of the language of science; but these criticisms should not be construed either as denying that logic is essentially syntax—for I think this is true—or as denying that syntactical treatment of some philosophical problems can be very fruitful. To account for this fruitfulness, however, it is no more necessary to suppose that these philosophical problems are themselves problems of syntax than it is necessary, in order to account for the power of arithmetic to anticipate in certain respects the outcome of physical operations, to suppose that these physical operations are themselves operations of arithmetic.[46]

---

[44] *F. L. M.*, p. 3.
[45] *Ibid.*, p. 4.
[46] Cf. "Symbols, Signs, and Signals," *loc. cit.*, pp. 50-52.

PART II

The Subject Matter and Method

of Philosophy

CHAPTER EIGHT

How Is the Subject Matter of Any Given
Systematic Inquiry Defined?

A NUMBER of recent hypotheses concerning the nature of
philosophy and the method appropriate to its tasks have
now been reviewed and criticized. The time has come to
state the hypothesis the writer himself would submit.

1. *Philosophy a Search for Knowledge.*—In common with most
of those already examined, the hypothesis I propose takes for
granted to begin with that philosophy is a knowledge-seeking
enterprise. In this respect, therefore, it holds that philosophy
resembles the natural and other sciences, and itself is, or seeks
to be, a science. This means that its utterances, like theirs,
claim to be in contrast with those of poets, priests, and
prophets; that its basic function is not to impart feelings or to
edify or to exhort, but to enlighten; that the task of its professors is to teach, not to preach; that the philosopher, like
the scientist, is not a pastor but an investigator.

The knowledge philosophy seeks will, it is true, have
bearings on man's ways of conducting his thoughts, his feelings, and his actions, for that knowledge is in part of the
kind itself called wisdom and in part of the kind that furnishes
the basis for a wisdom more secure than is otherwise to be
had. But the philosopher's wisdom, so far as he has such
knowledge, is not to be thought of as somehow innate in his

particular soul or as vouchsafed privately to him by special divine revelation. Rather, it derives from scientific study by him of the facts that are the subject matter distinctive of philosophy; and his search for knowledge is neither less nor more nor otherwise dependent on contact with concrete social or moral problems than the search for chemical or physical knowledge is dependent on contact with concrete engineering problems.

The knowledge philosophy seeks, moreover, is not knowledge in a different or less rigorous sense of the term than the knowledge sought by the other sciences. It too is knowledge as contrasted with guesses, articles of faith, snap judgments vague or unsupported opinions, prejudices, and wish-born beliefs. From this it follows that the method of philosophy must be no less scientific than that of any other knowledge-seeking enterprise, for "scientific" means nothing more and nothing less than knowledge-yielding.

But to say that the method of philosophy must be scientific does not imply either that philosophy must seek to borrow and to build upon the results of the other sciences, or that knowledge-yielding method will, as applied to philosophical problems, take the same specific forms as when applied to the problems of, for instance, physics or biology or even mathematics. For the specific devices which make for the attainment of knowledge in each of these sciences are dictated by the specific nature of the subject matter to be dealt with, and vary even as between one and another of these sciences. We may therefore expect that this will be the case also with philosophy. Thus, when the assertion is made here that the method of philosophy must be as scientific as that of these other sciences, what is meant is that philosophy must formulate its propositions with the same regard for unambiguity, must be as scrupulous in its verification of them, and must in-quire into their consequences and presuppositions as system-atically as does any other science. For these are characteristics that any inquiry, no matter into what, must have if it is to have any claim to being called scientific.

It may be urged, of course, that ethics, epistemology, aesthetics, etc., are not truly sciences because their procedure actually lacks these very characteristics. But to this I should reply that although it has indeed lacked them in considerable measure, these sciences are as yet only in their infancy, and that the infancy of all the sciences has been marked by methodological blundering. What defines a possible genuine science and distinguishes it from an impossible and neces-sarily spurious one is the existence both of a subject matter distinct from that of any other science, and of a method by which knowledge, properly so called, could be obtained about this subject matter if that method were employed. In the case of chemistry, for instance, the subject matter it now studies always existed, and the methods it now uses always were methods capable of yielding knowledge of it. This was true even in the days when both these methods and this sub-ject matter were only being groped for under the name of alchemy. Phrenology, on the other hand, probably is not a possible science because the correlations that constitute its assumed subject matter, viz., the correlations between the protuberances of the skull and the mental and emotional "faculties" of man, would seem to be in fact nonexistent.

Thus what is implied by calling ethics, epistemology, aesthetics, etc., sciences is not that they have already won knowledge in amounts comparable with, say, chemistry, or already have to a comparable extent acquired mastery of their appropriate methods, but only that, unlike phrenology, they are capable of becoming genuine sciences. This only means that (*a*) what they seek is knowledge, properly so called (*b*) concerning a subject matter that really exists and is distinctive of them, and (*c*) that there is a method, as yet not adequately mastered by them, which it if were employed would yield genuine knowledge concerning their subject matter.

2. *The Claim of Philosophy to a Subject matter Distinctively Its Own.*—A question as to the structure of the hydrogen atom is, by common consent, not a philosophical but a physical question. And, contrariwise, a question as to the relation of philosophy to natural science, or as to the difference between falsity and error and the relation of each to truth, would commonly be classed as a philosophical question and not as one belonging to any of the natural sciences. But since employment of a method truly scientific cannot, as already pointed out, be what distinguishes these sciences from philosophy—while, as this example shows, we do distinguish between questions belonging to them and questions belonging to philosophy—the basis of distinction can only consist in a difference of subject matter. What then is the subject matter distinctive of philosophy?

To answer this difficult question it will be useful as a first step to ask ourselves what general form an answer to a question of this kind necessarily takes in any other case—for instance, in the easier case of the natural sciences. But, to forestall misunderstandings, let us agree at the outset that by the "formal" sciences will be meant pure logic and pure mathematics, and by the "natural" sciences, all the sciences that study what has commonly been called nature or the material world. The latter will thus comprise, for instance, the physical sciences—physics, chemistry, astronomy, etc., and also the biological sciences, including not only the zoological and botanical sciences, but also psychology of the physiological and behavioristic kinds. The natural sciences, moreover, will include also the social sciences—sociology, economics, political economy—in so far as these are treated as studies of the behavior and practices of men in the mass or in social situations. On the other hand, in so far as the social sciences attempt to discover which social, political, or economic institutions are good, or are best under given circumstances, I would class them as applied ethics and therefore with the philosophical sciences. As "mental" sciences I would class psychology of the introspective kind, and other sciences, if any, also based on introspection but dealing with questions not ordinarily considered in what has gone by the name of introspective psychology.

History is usually classed with the social sciences, as concerning itself with human societies or human activities in their time dimension, but there is of course also such a thing as the history of the solar system, of a given tree or a given river, etc. Thus, "history" is not the name of any particular subject matter, but rather of a dimension of the study of anything that exists in time. For example, we may study the history of the earth, for the earth exists in time; but we may also study the history of the study of the earth, that is, the history of geology; or the history of mathematics, of philosophy, of art, etc., for all these human activities extend through time. On the other hand, the historian who may seek to explain, for example, the decline of the Roman Empire, is not relieved of the need for this purpose of a knowledge of, among other things, the laws of economics or of social psychology, by the fact that the events he deals with happened long ago and are known with much less detail than are contemporary events of a similar kind. For in so far as he attempts explanation or generalization, he is speaking in his capacity (if he has any) as economist, political scientist, social psychologist, etc., rather than in his capacity as historian—although, of course, the facts he explains or generalizes are facts that he or others have ascertained in their capacity as historians.[1]

3. *Primitive and Derivative Facts.*—Returning now to the question of the subject matter that distinguishes the group of sciences we call the natural sciences from other scientific inquiries, to say as we did above that what they study is nature or the material world only brings up the question as to what exactly differentiates "nature" from whatever we contrast it with. And it is not easy to find a definition of nature that will apply equally to things seemingly as heterogeneous as light and heat, the mechanisms of heredity, the mating displays of the Australian bower bird, the varieties of subatomic particles, the relation between supply and demand, the differences in basal metabolism among different races, etc., all of which belong to the realm which the natural sciences investigate. A solution of the difficulty becomes discernible only when it occurs to us to make a certain highly important distinction—namely, that between what we may call the primitive facts of a science and its derivative facts.

The primitive facts of a given science are those which, for it, are beyond question. They are, on the one hand, the facts about which the science asks its very first, most elementary questions, and on the other hand, the facts—of the same general kind—to which the science ultimately appeals in testing the validity of its hypotheses. The primitive facts of

---

[1] Sciences such as the social sciences or, in certain of its aspects, astronomy, in which experimentation is wholly or mostly impracticable, are much more closely dependent than others on the history of their objects for the facts on which to base their inductive generalizations. The facts, for example, on which Kepler had to depend for his discovery of the laws of planetary motion consisted chiefly of a historical record, viz., the record made by Tycho Brahe of the positions at given times of the planet Mars.

a science are thus facts of the kind with which its inquiries originate and also terminate. An example of a fact which for physics is primitive, and which originates inquiry, would be the rising and falling of the tide. That the tide does rise and fall is perceptually obvious at many places and is therefore not questioned; but about it many questions occur to the physicist. Other facts primitive in the same sense for a physicist would be, on certain occasions, that a given string is stretched; that he plucks it; that a sound occurs; that a certain stretched string is longer than a certain other; that certain metal filings are clinging to a certain metal bar; that a certain body is moving, etc. On many occasions the physicist would regard such facts as established beyond question by ordinary perceptual observation; but many questions about them would arise in his mind.

On the other hand, examples of primitive facts functioning in certain cases as terminative rather than as originative of physical inquiries would be that a certain pointer is at a certain place on a graduated scale; that on a certain occasion no sound occurs when a given bell is struck; that on a certain occasion two falling bodies do not reach the ground at the same time, etc. Obviously, no primitive fact is intrinsically originative or intrinsically terminative. The distinction is purely functional, being only a matter of whether a question is being asked about, or on the contrary answered by, a given primitive fact. The same primitive fact might thus function at one time as originative of an inquiry and at another time as terminative of a different inquiry.

The derivative facts of a given science, on the other hand, are those discovered as a result of the attempt to answer, about its primitive facts, the kind of questions that distinguish an enterprise of the sort called scientific from enterprises of other sorts. These questions concern relations of the given facts to one another, and, more specifically, relations capable of providing a basis for inferences from given facts to other facts in the field of the given science. The nature of the problems formulated in the questions distinctive of the kind of enterprise called a science may thus be described broadly by saying that they are problems of analysis and synthesis of the facts with which the given science is concerned.

The problem of discovering an empirical law, for instance, is a problem both of analysis and of synthesis. Starting with several groups of primitive facts, the discovery requires, on the one hand, abstraction from all except certain common features of the facts of a given group, and, on the other hand, detection of a connection or correlation between such features of one group and similarly abstracted features of the other groups. Both the connection or correlation constituting the law, and the abstracted features themselves, which it relates, are thus derivative from—i.e., were implicitly present in—the primitive facts among which they were detected. Words such as temperature, weight, size, shape, motion, velocity, acceleration, etc., are examples of names of derivatives from certain groups of physical primitives; and very early in the development of physics the questions asked are directly about facts already derived from the physical primitives, and are thus only indirectly about the latter. The attempt at further analysis and synthesis of such derivative facts as these operations have already brought to light leads sooner or later to the construction of theories. These are devices which, through the postulation, as implicit in the primitive facts, of features not detectable in them by abstractive observation, permit the carrying of the task of analysis and synthesis farther than is possible through direct observation alone, no matter how minutely discriminative. For the postulated features make possible the formulation of laws themselves making possible the prediction of certain primitive facts which, if later observed to be as predicted, contribute to validate—or if not as predicted, suffice to invalidate—those laws. Additional examples of terms, again from physics, which themselves name derivative facts and which enter into the formulation of such derivatives as laws and theories, would be magnetic field, atom, proton, electric charge, electric potential, energy, etc. The distinction between the originative and terminative roles, already made among primitive facts, applies to derivative facts also, but only in a relative and proximate sense, not in an absolute and ultimate one as in the case of primitive facts.

4. *Definition of the Subject Matter Distinctive of a Given Science.*—In the light of the distinction now made between the primitive and the derivative facts of a given science, we may say that the subject matter distinctive of a given science consists of all facts that are primitive for it, plus any facts analytically or synthetically derivative from these and about which further problems of analysis or synthesis may arise. Or, because the derivative facts of a given science can be said to belong to its subject matter only because they are derivative from the primitives of specifically that science, we can say more briefly that what ultimately distinguishes one science from others is the nature of its primitive facts.

With this distinction as between the primitive and the derivative facts of a given science we may compare Loewenberg's distinction between pre-analytical and post analytical data.[2] I cannot decide whether or not my distinction is essentially identical with his, but it is at least similar. His distinction emphasizes analysis to the neglect of synthesis, but

---

[2] *Jour. of Phil.*, XXIV, No. 1 (Jan., 1927).

he has since indicated that this was no part of its essential intent.[3] In the later paper, however, he rewords his distinction as one between "data of acquiescence" and "data of transformation," and this does not seem to be the same distinction as the one I intend when I speak of primitive and derivative facts, for the latter are not transformations of the former in the sense—apparently intended by Loewenberg—in which a statue can be described as a transformation of a marble block. For creation or invention is one thing, and discovery is another; and derivative facts are not made by man but discovered by him through analysis and synthesis. What is begotten by man through these operations is not changes in the facts initially given[4] but changes in man's knowledge. A man's knowledge—i.e., the fact that he has knowledge and what its extent is—is indeed in part an "artifact of reason"; but the facts themselves which he knows are not artifacts of reason but discoveries (in part) of reason. The only exception would be the facts also known by him which consist of the very instruments of reasoning (e.g., logical or mathematical) that he himself has created.

The illustrations of primitive and derivative facts given in the preceding section serve to call attention to something very important to notice in the present connection. It is that not only in physics but also in any other science the overwhelming majority of the propositions asserted as results of its inquiries are explicitly and directly not about its primitive but about its derivative facts; and because of this it may easily seem not only to the outsider but still more to the practitioner of the science that such facts as are constituted by the derivatives are what the science is really about. But

---

[3] "Artifacts of Reason," *University of California Publications in Philosophy*, XXI (1931), 51.

[4] Cf.: "The facts of nature undergo transformation by taking the impress of man's refined concepts and categories," *ibid.*, p. 54.

just because these are known at all only derivatively from the primitive (and more vulgar) facts, and indeed, as noted above, have claim to belong to the given science only because they are derivative from the primitives of specifically that science, these primitives, although seldom explicitly mentioned in the assertions embodying the results reached by the science, are nevertheless what all its assertions are ultimately about. That is, these assertions, although directly and explicitly about derivatives, are indirectly and implicitly about the primitives, in the sense that they are analytic or synthetic "functions" having the primitives as "arguments." This is shown by the fact that any of the derivative assertions—let us say the assertion "if A, then B"—can be expressed in some such form as: "Primitives P, P', P″, etc., are such that analysis or synthesis of them (in such and such a way) exhibits in them a constituent which is such that if A, then B."

This means that the subject matter distinctive of a given science is, in ultimate analysis, defined by the very ones among its facts which it least often explicitly mentions in the statements of its results. To remember this will help us in our attempt to discern the nature of the primitive facts distinctive of philosophy.

CHAPTER NINE

The Subject Matter of the Natural, the Formal, and the Mental Sciences

IN THE light of the conclusions reached in the preceding chapter, the problem of defining the subject matter distinctive of the natural sciences as a group is now seen to reduce to that of identifying the sort of facts primitive for these sciences.

1. *The Subject Matter Distinctive of the Natural Sciences.*— I submit that the primitive facts of the natural sciences are any facts ascertainable by ordinary external perception; that is, any facts susceptible of being perceptually public in the sense that ordinary perceptual observation is what establishes them as beyond question for all the practitioners of those sciences. That it is facts of this sort which originate and also terminate inquiry in the case of physics is obvious from an examination of the examples of primitive facts of this science that have been given; and the case is the same with the primitive facts of the other natural sciences. All these sciences both start from and in the last resort appeal to "observation" or "experience"; and in their case this observation or experience is observation of the ordinary, externally perceptual kind; for only facts susceptible of being observed in this way are susceptible of being directly identified or observed by

several persons, that is, are susceptible of being observationally public.

That facts of the perceptually public kind are those with which natural scientists start, and to which they ultimately appeal as verificatory or confutative, is widely recognized among them, and on occasion they themselves explicitly declare it. As clear-cut a statement of this sort as I have found would be the following: "An essential characteristic of all facts admitted to the body of scientific knowledge is that they are *public*. Science demands public rather than private facts. . . . . Science deals only with those aspects of nature which all normal men can observe alike."[1] Another statement substantially to the same effect is the following: "The subject matter of science may be defined as those immediate judgments concerning which universal agreement can be obtained."[2] But what the practitioners of the natural sciences do testifies even more eloquently than what they say that the facts which for them are primitive in the sense we have assigned to that term are facts of the perceptually public kind.

This does not mean, however, that anything to which ordinary external perception may appear to testify is necessarily accepted as a primitive fact by natural science, for there are such things as perceptual illusions, and even perhaps also collective hallucinations. We can hardly engage here in a discussion of the difference between veridical and nonveridical perception; but it must be pointed out at least that although in given cases we may doubt the factuality of what perceptual observation appears to reveal, we cannot doubt it in every case without wholly depriving the natural sciences of their subject matter.

---

[1] S. S. Stevens, "The Operational Basis of Psychology," *American Journal of Psychology*, XLVII (April, 1935), 327.

[2] N. Campbell, *Physics, the Elements*, p. 21.

The reason for this is that there is no such thing as a problem or question without data. The data of a problem are the facts it is about; and to say that a problem which is not just hypothetical but categorical is about facts perceptually public is to say that these facts are given categorically and not just hypothetically. If in a given case the data of the problem turn out not to be facts, but to have been only erroneously believed to be facts, then in that case no categorical problem is left, but, if any at all, only a speculative one.[3]

In the light of these considerations, I submit that we may now conclude that nature—which is the subject matter of the natural sciences as a group—consists of such facts as are susceptible of being perceptually public, plus such facts as are analytically or synthetically implicit in these.

2. *The Subject Matter Distinctive of the Formal Sciences.*— The distinction between primitive and derivative facts applies to the formal sciences as well as to the natural, but the primitive facts of the formal sciences are of a different sort.

The facts to which these sciences ultimately appeal, and with which they start, are always of the nature of prescriptive verbal definitions, or postulates, or rules of formation or transformation. These obviously are not facts which the logician or mathematician finds, but facts which he creates by means of stipulations or prescriptions. But the primitives of the formal sciences do not include all facts so created. For example, that a given child's name is John is a fact created by his parents through a prescriptive act, but the fact so created does not belong to pure logic, since it contains as a constituent the child himself, who is not a logical entity but a physical one of flesh and blood. The prescription

---

[3] Cf. M. Cohen, *op. cit.*, pp. 86 f.

that creates a fact of this sort may be described as a rei-verbal one; and the prescription, of the converse sort, by which for instance the inhabitants of a city assign an incumbent to the description "mayor of the city" may be called a verbo-real prescription. As distinguished from either of these, the prescriptions which create the primitive facts of the formal sciences always are of the verbo-verbal sort. That is, the primitive facts of these sciences are created, by means of stipulations, wholly out of what we may call discursive or verbal entities.

Discursive entities are any entities fulfilling the following conditions:

1. They are susceptible of being readily uttered, whether vocally, graphically, or otherwise; that is, they are such that a perceptible utterance of them can ordinarily be caused by the mere wish.

2. They are recognizable as the same in the various utterances of them, whether these be graphic, vocal, or other; or we may put this also by saying that their various utterances are recognizable as "equal."[4]

3. They are entities the utterances of which are always man-caused, artifactual—never, or virtually never, caused by natural events independently of the activity of man.[5]

It is wholly immaterial to the problems of the pure formal sciences whether the discursive entities of which they make use do or do not symbolize or stand for entities other than discursive. The postulates, definitions, and rules they take as their primitive facts can therefore be any whatever that they please.[6] A limitation upon the possibility of completely

---

[4] Cf. Carnap, *L. S. L.*, p. 15.

[5] A fuller discussion of discursive entities may be found in "Symbols, Signs, and Signals," *loc. cit.*, pp. 43 ff.

[6] But of course the primitives chosen must be things truly having the nature of postulates, definitions, rules.

arbitrary choice of such primitives enters only when pragmatic considerations are introduced, that is, when applicability of the calculus based on the primitives to the solution of problems concerning entities other than those of the given calculus is a desideratum.

The derivative facts of the formal sciences, which we may call their theorems (as distinguished from their definitions, postulates, and rules), consist of the expressions that may be derived from such primitives by means of the very rules these primitives include.

The knowledge given us by the formal sciences is a priori knowledge because the truth-value of their propositions is determined wholly by prescription. But although in all cases their truth-value is so determined, knowledge of their truth-value may be direct or indirect. It is direct whenever we are laying down the postulates, definitions, or rules; but it is only indirect in the case of the theorems, since their truth-value, although implicit in that of those primitives, becomes known to us only in so far as we discover it through deduction of the theorems from the primitives.

3. *The Subject Matter Distinctive of the Mental Sciences.*—As stated above when we listed the sciences to be designated respectively as natural, formal, and mental, the latter comprise psychology of the genuinely introspective sort, and other sciences, if any, which also take as their primitives the facts revealed by introspection, but which ask about them questions going beyond those that have usually been considered under the heading of "introspective psychology." The derivative facts of the science of mind will, like those of any other science, be facts analytically or synthetically implicit in its primitives; that is, they will consist of relations in which the primitives stand to one another. To clarify the

scope of the science of mind as distinguished from that of
what has gone by the name of "introspective psychology,"
it is necessary to point to some questions, traditionally considered by psychologists of the introspectionist school, which
do not strictly belong to the science of mind; and to some
questions, not usually considered by these psychologists,
which nevertheless do belong to it.

4. *Some Questions Dealt with by "Introspectionists" Not
within the Scope of the Science of Mind.*—An idea of the sorts
of facts that introspective psychologists have brought to
light may be gained by examination of such a textbook as
that of the late Edward B. Titchener, who may be taken as a
representative introspectionist. We notice first that the
larger portion of its contents is not concerned with the
analysis or synthesis of introspectables, i.e., with investigation of the relations of introspectables to one another, but
with the physical conditions under which certain kinds of
introspectable facts—chiefly sensations—occur. Although
it is very useful for purposes of introspective study to know
these physical conditions, so that we may reproduce at will
the introspectables depending on them which we desire to
study, *discovery* of these physical conditions is of course
strictly speaking no part of the task of introspective psychology but of psychophysics or psychophysiology. The content
of a science of mind, as represented by the pages devoted to
introspective psychology proper in Titchener's textbook,
would be rather meager, for about all it would include would
be an inventory of the kinds of sensations and other mental
states, an account of certain of the elements and dimensions of
some complex kinds of mental states, and an account of the
general laws in accordance with which mental elements become discriminated or submerged, dissociated or associated.

As Titchener himself suggests, a science of mind limited to this "would stand to scientific psychology very much as the old-fashioned natural histories stand to modern textbooks of biology."[7] A scientific psychology, he declares, must not only describe but also explain.

5. *Artificial Limitations of the Scope of the Science of Mind.*— However, without mentioning any other ground than that "with change of our surroundings, entirely new consciousnesses may be set up," Titchener sweepingly asserts that "we cannot regard one mental process as the cause of another mental process." And since he also assumes, without argument, that we cannot "regard nervous processes as the cause of mental processes," he concludes that explanation of mental processes consists in tracing correspondences between them and nervous processes: "The nervous system does not cause, but it does explain mind. It explains mind as the map of a country explains the fragmentary glimpses of hills and rivers and towns that we catch on our journey through it."[8] I submit first that if this is explanation at all, which is very questionable, it is certainly not explanation in the sense in which the term is used in the other sciences, where it means either the tracing of effects to their causes, or the deduction of known empirical laws from theoretical constructs. And, second, the search for correlations between psychical and physiological processes is in any case not introspective psychology but, as already pointed out, psychophysiology.

Further, as regards Titchener's assumption that no mental process can cause another nor therefore explain another, I submit that on the contrary such causation is just what we do have in any case of association of ideas. Imagining something, or thinking of something, does in numberless instances

---

[7] *A Textbook of Psychology*, p. 38.
[8] *Ibid.*, p. 39.

cause the occurrence of some other mental event—of some other image, of the thought of something else, of some emotion or some impulse, etc., as the case may be. The sight or image of a little cross, for example, causes to arise the thought of addition, or of Christianity, or of a crossroad, etc., according to the contextual content of the mind at the time. Thinking of the approach of black clouds causes the thought of rain, and belief that black clouds are approaching causes belief that rain is imminent, etc. The fact that we believe rain to be imminent is properly and adequately explained by the fact that we believe black clouds are approaching, or that we feel rheumatic pains, or that we believe the barometer is falling, etc. Investigation of the associations of ideas habitual to a given mind—that is, of the ideas regularly caused in it by given ideas—is what investigation of the given mind chiefly consists in; and establishing valuable connections of this sort between ideas or other kinds of mental states is what constitutes education of a mind. Each such regular connection constitutes a property or law of the mind in which it exists, and it is a part of the task of a comprehensive science of mind to investigate minds in respect to such properties.

Titchener's assumption that no mental process can cause another mental process is thus too sweeping. What is true is that mental processes of the kind called sensations are not generally, if ever, directly caused by other mental processes. But the causes of mental processes other than sensations generally are other mental processes (whether themselves sensations or something else). Titchener's assumption therefore constitutes an artificial limitation of the scope of the science of mind.

There is another limitation which introspectionists generally have imposed on that science just as gratuitously, that, namely, introduced by the assumption that there can be no facts in mind other than those introspection can reveal. It is based on the erroneous belief that an "unconscious mental fact" is synonymous with an "unconscious state of consciousness," the latter being obviously a contradiction in terms. As against this, I submit that the mental facts introspection directly discloses are only those that are primitive for the science of mind, and that its derivative facts are discovered not directly by introspective observation but, as in any other science, by analysis and synthesis of the facts observation itself reveals.

To see how arbitrary is the assumption that there can be no facts in mind other than those introspection reveals, we need only consider what would be the parallel assumption in the case of nature. It would be that there can be no facts in nature other than those susceptible of being perceptually observed. As already pointed out, however, the vast majority of the facts revealed by the natural sciences are not directly perceptible at all. Many of them are accepted as facts, and as facts in nature, only because postulation of them enables us to deduce facts in nature already perceived or laws of nature already discovered inductively, and additional ones that turn out to be verified by further observations of nature. In every property or law, for instance, which, on the basis of observations, we assert as inhering in things, there is an element of postulation just as truly as in our assertions that such entities as atoms or electrons exist; for a statement of the laws or properties of things is not a statement merely of how they have been observed to behave in specified circumstances, but also of how they can be expected to behave again in similar circumstances. But that their behavior will the *next* time be as before is of course always something that at the given time we have not yet observed but only postulate.

I submit that in the science of mind we have exactly as good a right, and the very same sort of right, to postulate and to call mental certain entities which introspection does not directly disclose at all, but which similarly enable us to deduce facts which introspection has already revealed and additional ones that introspection eventually verifies. Examples of such entities would be the countless opinions, beliefs, mental associations, memories, etc., which all of us have, but of the having which we are totally unconscious at most times. They are properties of our minds, and our minds possess them even at times when they are not introspectively manifest, just as the physical property called combustibility, for instance, is possessed by this sheet of paper even at times, such as the present, when this property is not manifest to perceptual observation. The realm of mind, like that of nature, includes all the facts derivative from its primitives, and thus includes vastly more than is ever directly revealed by observation of it.

6. *Gestalt Psychology.*—To what has been said above concerning introspective psychology it must be added that gestalt psychologists question the validity of the sort of introspective analysis which Titchener and others give of, e.g., the perception of distance in terms of doubleness of images, relatively blurred or sharp definition, accommodation sensations, etc. They deny the possibility of analysis of perception into such elements, and phrase their own account in terms of "organization," "forces of organization," "factors of organization," "stresses and strains in a psychophysical field," etc., borrowing the latter concept from physics, and in turn asserting that in physics, as in psychology, fundamental processes are molar rather than molecular. But in view of the insistence of gestalt psychology on the

analogy between psychology and physics, and of the indubitable and enormous fruitfulness in the latter of analysis in terms of "molecular" entities such as molecules, atoms, electrons, etc., denial of the possibility, in psychology, of analysis into elementary mental constituents has been one of the most vulnerable points of gestalt psychology. And what it proposes instead is at times hard to distinguish from "explanations" of the automatic and easy type illustrated by the famous example of the *vis dormitiva*.

The chief contributions of gestalt psychology seem to me, for one thing, its broader conception of introspection as including observation of what it calls the "behavioral environment," i.e., observation of the nature of the environment which at a given time we believe ourselves (whether erroneously or rightly) to be facing. Our "behavioral environment" thus consists of what Broad calls our "epistemological objects" as distinguished from "ontological objects," to which the former may or may not correspond. But perhaps the most significant contribution of gestalt psychology has been its insistence on the importance of wholes of experience, that is, on the importance of the experiential context in which a given bit of experience occurs. The necessity of taking this context into account explicitly would have been obvious from the start to anyone who realized that the causal relation—whether in a given case its terms happen to be psychical or physical—is essentially not a two-term but a three-term relation: one term, a given set of circumstances; another term, a given change in them (this change being the cause-event); and the third term, the further change in them (this being the effect-event) resulting from the cause-event. A causal law is thus never, as so often seems to be assumed, of the form "any event of kind C causes an event of kind E," but always of the form "a change of kind C in circumstances of kind K always causes in them a further change of kind E." The taking into account of wholes of experience by gestalt psychology seems to me to amount to introducing into the methodology of introspective psychology the sort of practice which an adequate realization of the general nature of the causal relation would dictate for the methodology of any field where this relation figures.

From the subject matter of, respectively, the natural, the formal, and the mental sciences, let us now pass to that of the philosophical sciences.

CHAPTER TEN

The Subject Matter Distinctive of Philosophy

I now submit that the facts primitive for philosophy all consist of appraisals or, as I propose to say indifferently, valuations.

1. *The Primitives of Philosophy.*—But when it is asserted both that the facts primitive for philosophy are appraisals, and that the facts primitive for a science are those it takes as subjects of its questions but as not themselves in question, it is not meant that the justice or warrantedness of appraisals is in general beyond question for philosophy. What is for it beyond question is their occurrence, i.e., that certain appraisals are made of certain entities by certain persons.

Appraisals are of many kinds and so are the things appraised. The latter include not only objects, events, or situations external to man, but also man's own experiences, and his activities and operations, whether physical, psychical, or other. Among kinds of appraisals, some of the more familiar are those we formulate (when we formulate them at all) by means of such adjectives as "good" and "bad," "right" and "wrong," "moral" and "immoral," "beautiful" and "ugly," "sublime" and "ridiculous," "sound" and "erroneous," "veridical" and "illusory," "valid" and "fallacious," "real" and "unreal," "sacred" and "profane," etc., and by means of the comparatives (if any) of such adjectives.[1]

To appraise something is thus to judge its merits or worth —positive or negative, comparative or absolute. That any appraisal is either positive or negative is I believe the very essence of appraisal; that is, generically, appraising is nothing more and nothing less than "yea-ing" or "nay-ing." The yea or nay—the positive or negative judgment—may be dominantly emotional (e.g., a liking or disliking) or dominantly epistemic (e.g., a believing or disbelieving) or dominantly volitional (e.g., an effort to cause or to prevent). But in all cases the appraising consists of some form of favoring or disfavoring response to the entity appraised.[2] The adjectives of appraisal accordingly go in pairs and the members of each pair are opposites. Which pair of specific adjectives is relevant in a given case depends on the kind of entity being appraised and on the general type of interest one takes in it. For example, if the entity to be appraised is an opinion, and the interest taken in it epistemic, the adjectives "erroneous" and "sound" would be relevant. If the interest is emotional, adjectives such as "shocking" or "agreeable" would be relevant. If the entity appraised is an inference instead of an opinion, and the interest in it epistemic, then the adjectives "fallacious" and "valid" would be relevant, etc.

2. *Appraisal and Description.*—When we say of a certain fabric, for instance, that it is blue or tightly woven or light-

---

[1] "To formulate" is used throughout in the sense of "to express by means of conventional symbols." These are usually words. The words used in the formulation may but need not be uttered. Utterances of them may be vocal, graphic, or other.

[2] "Entity" is used throughout in the broad sense of "something," not in the narrow one of "substance" or "object" as contrasted with "situation," "event," "activity," etc.

weight, we are said to be describing it; whereas if we say that it is beautiful or good or useful, we are said to be stating an appraisal of it. But it may be objected that these appraisals are themselves descriptions. For instance, to say that the fabric is beautiful means, perhaps, that it is such as to cause, in persons who contemplate it aesthetically, feelings that are pleasant; to say that it is useful may mean that it is an effective means to purposes of certain sorts, etc. These statements, just as much as the statement that the fabric is blue or tightly woven, describe characteristics the fabric possesses that distinguish it from certain other fabrics. Again, the police description of an escaped criminal may include not only statements of his height and weight, of the color of his eyes and hair, etc., but also a statement that he is, perhaps, good-looking.

The contrasting of valuation or appraisal on the one hand with description on the other thus seems hard to defend, for to describe something is to state the characters it has, no matter of what sort. On this account, the contrast really intended would probably be better expressed as one between statement of value-characters and statement of characters other than these; that is, as a contrast between descriptions that formulate appraisals and descriptions that do not.

It is important to note that the two may consist of the very same words, although when the words state an appraisal they mean something additional to what they mean when intended to describe without appraising. To say of a novel that it is very long, for instance, is to state a character it has, but whether this is statement merely of an objective character, or in addition of an adverse appraisal, depends on whether the character mentioned is assumed to be objectionable—disvalued or demeritorious. Again, one might say of a painting that in it the volume aspect of the objects it represents, and the relations in the third dimension of space of these objects to one another, are emphasized. This is to state merely an objective character of the painting, if the character mentioned is not being offered as ground for liking or disliking or for admiring or condemning the painting. Otherwise the statement is not only objectively descriptive but also descriptive of the utterer's appraisal of the painting. If the painting is a mural and emphasis of the third dimension is something disliked in a mural by the person speaking, his statement that the painting has this character constitutes adverse criticism of the painting. From the same person, however, the very same statement, but concerning an easel painting, might express favorable criticism.

A statement of appraisal, then, and a "merely descriptive" statement are distinguished by the fact that the latter does not, but the former does, express (whether explicitly or implicitly) a valuing (positive or negative) of the entity about which it is made.[3]

3. *Appraisals Primitive for Philosophy Spontaneous, Particular, and Formulated.*—Although all facts primitive for philosophy are appraisals, not all appraisals are philosophical primitives. Appraisals expressible in the form "anything of kind K has value V" are obtained either by induction from particular appraisals or by deduction from some theory, and are therefore derivative, not primitive. Hence, primitive appraisals are particular, not general. But not even all particular appraisals are philosophical primitives, for a particular appraisal may be made deductively from a theory, and cannot then serve as material or evidence for or against that theory or any rival one. To be primitive, an appraisal

---

[3] The entity valued may be valued either for what it immediately is, or as a means or obstacle to something so valued, or both.

must therefore be not only particular but also spontaneous, in the sense of not deduced from any theory. Particular appraisals which are simply automatic imitations of those of other persons in one's environment are not spontaneous either, in the sense in which spontaneity is a requirement for philosophical primitiveness; for even if the appraisals of which they are imitations are themselves spontaneous, the imitations of them do not constitute additional bases for generalizations or theories, any more than the images of a given biological specimen in half a dozen mirrors would provide half a dozen additional specimens.

But further, if the generalizations and theories of philosophy are to have scientific status—are to constitute knowledge in as genuine a sense as, for instance, those of the natural sciences—then philosophical generalizations and theories must likewise be testable by other persons beside those who propound them. This requires that the spontaneous particular appraisals which are generalized and theorized about, and by reference to which the validity of the generalizations and theories is to be tested, shall be known to these other persons. This is possible only if they are expressed, and expressed in public and commonly understood symbols; for, unlike the primitive facts of natural science, appraisals themselves are not exhibitable to public perception. The entity appraised sometimes is so exhibitable, but the appraisal made of it never is. The appraisal is a subjective fact and can therefore be made known to persons other than the appraiser himself only through public utterance by him of some commonly understood symbol of it. The symbols consisting of the various adjectives of appraisal of ordinary language are the most usual and generally the only adequate medium available for the public expression of appraisals. The pair of words "yes" and "no," or their equivalents, may as already suggested be regarded as the *summum genus* of pairs of terms of appraisal.

How language for the communication of subjective facts, such as appraisals, is possible, is an interesting question but one that need not be taken up here. We only assume here, as common sense does, that such language exists; and that when we study appraisals, the entities we are studying are not the utterances themselves of any of the words of that language, but the subjective—not perceptually public—entities which certain of the words of that language stand for.

In the light of the foregoing remarks, some of which will be amplified in succeeding chapters, we may now summarily define the facts primitive for philosophy as consisting of such appraisals as are particular, spontaneous, and stated.

4. *Philosophical Theorizing Born of the Desire to Settle Doubts of Our Appraisals Rationally.*—That the facts primitive for philosophy—the facts it is ultimately about—are appraisals, is suggested by the nature of the occasions upon which thinking of the kind generally called philosophical spontaneously arises. They are occasions when our appraisals conflict among themselves or with those of other persons, or are hesitant, or otherwise come to be put in doubt, and where the conflict or doubt is not due to inadequate observation or description of the thing appraised.

This qualification is important, for the demand that arises in us for knowledge adequate to settle a doubt of an appraisal is satisfiable sometimes in one and sometimes in the other of two ways. What is needed to settle the doubt is in some cases better knowledge of what characters are actually possessed by the entity appraised; whereas in other cases it is better knowledge of characters which, if any entity possessed them, would warrant the sort of appraisal we are making. The distinction is essentially that between knowing better an entity we are talking about, and knowing better what we are saying about it—in this case, between knowing better the nature of the entity appraised, and knowing better the nature of the sort of appraisal we make of it.

For example, doubt as to whether something that a person did on a certain occasion was wrong may arise either from our not knowing exactly enough what he did do, or from our not knowing exactly enough what wrongness consists in. In cases of the first sort, the sort of knowledge needed is not philosophical. It is of the sort obtainable by more careful observation or description of the entity appraised. In cases of the second sort, the knowledge needed is of the kind which an adequate theory of appraisals of the sort made would provide. Such knowledge is philosophical: a theory of appraisals of the sort expressible by the adjective "wrong" would be an ethical theory; by the adjective "erroneous," an epistemological theory; by the adjective "beautiful," an aesthetic theory; by the adjective "real," an ontological theory, etc.

One or two concrete illustrations will make clear that situations of the kind described automatically generate philosophizing in rational persons.

Let us suppose that at a meeting of a college faculty the curriculum is under discussion, and that difference of opinion arises as to whether a given course ought or ought not to be required of all students—or, to put the same thing in other words, as to whether the requiring of this course for all students is a good or a bad thing to do. It may be that the disagreement arises only from misconceptions by some members of the faculty as to the content or the method of the course. If so, the point at issue is not philosophical, and more adequate information as to the nature of the course suffices to eliminate the conflict of appraisals. But if the nature of the course is equally well known to all and the conflict of appraisals is not at bottom only a conflict of vested interests in the curriculum, then it is one between latent philosophies of college education. The conceptions of what the nature, the methods, or the effects of a college education must be if it is to be good may hitherto have remained unformulated, and therefore more or less vague and fluid, or even wholly absent, in the minds of some members of the faculty. But the conflict of appraisals crystallizes or generates them and brings them to formulation. Thus, one member of the faculty may defend his condemnation of the proposal to prescribe the course by saying, perhaps, that the information it imparts to the student is very unlikely ever to be useful to him later; while another member will acknowledge this fact but declare it irrelevant, and approve the course perhaps on the ground that it provides a unique sort of intellectual discipline, or that it opens to the student a horizon of cultural if not of practical interest otherwise likely to remain closed to him.

Or, to take other examples, challenge of a person's condemnation of a novel may elicit from him the reason that the novel has a tragic ending—that is, the theory that a novel with a tragic ending is, other things being equal, inferior to one with a happy ending. A physician's refusal to perform an operation that would save the life of a monstrously malformed infant may be judged morally wrong by one person and morally right by another—the one defending his appraisal, perhaps, by appeal to the injunctions in the scriptures of his religion, and the other by appeal to the fact that useless suffering is avoided by allowing the infant to die.

Obviously, the reason offered by each person in defense of his appraisal constitutes the embryo, or a fragment, of a philosophy of the subject concerned. The defense consists in exhibiting the proposal in dispute as a case of a certain general kind, it being assumed that whatever is of this general kind commends itself—or, it may be, condemns itself—too evidently to need assertion, much less argument, of the appraisal. In most impromptu disputes, however, these implicit major premises of the appraisals made have not been thought of prior to the dispute, still less formulated. Rather, they are picked out of the dialectical air at the moment, as being prima facie both plausible and logically adequate to support the appraisal made. But as soon as they are formulated—put into words—critical scrutiny of them becomes possible not only to our opponents but also to ourselves, for our opinions are proof against doubt by ourselves only so long as they retain the status of tacit assumptions. The moment we assert them, question of them thrusts itself upon us, even if we then immediately find ourselves able to meet the question with a confident reassertion. Often, however, scrutiny of the hitherto tacit but now formulated major premises of our appraisals exhibits ambiguities or brings to mind cases the formulation has intended to include—or, as the case may be, to exclude—but which it does not, or reveals incompatibility between the major premise formulated and others to which one has already committed one's self. Whether these defects be pointed out by opponents or discovered by ourselves, they call for remedy through definitions of terms, and often also of the terms in which these definitions are framed; or through introduction or removal of restrictions to make those major premises cover all and none but the sorts of cases we intend; or through distinctions adequate to render them compatible with one's other commitments, etc.

But to do all this thoroughly and with exactness is to formulate a comprehensive philosophy of the subject in view—a theory of the sort of appraisal concerned—in the light of which it will be evident whether the appraisal we made was sound or erroneous. It may be, of course, that the defects which opponents believe they discern in the premises we advance for our appraisal are not really there. But that they are not there can be shown only by means of an apparatus of definitions, classifications, distinctions, etc., adequate to exhibit the confusions, misunderstandings, or false assumptions upon which the objections were based—that is, again, by means of a comprehensive philosophy of the subject in view.

5. *The Derivative Part of the Subject Matter of Philosophy the More Prominent and Technical.*—The generalizations themselves, and also the definitions, classifications, operations, etc., by means of which theories explanatory of the generalizations are constructed and tested, are derivative facts, not primitive; and in philosophy as elsewhere they quickly bulk larger and more prominently, and are more technical, than the primitives. Because of this, their derivative relation to the homely and untechnical primitives is easily lost sight of and the technical subject matter is mistakenly regarded as self-contained. Yet the technical problems with which philosophers are so largely occupied are, as in any other science, generated solely by the persistent attempt to analyze and synthetize in a thoroughgoing manner the humble primitive facts. They are marked off as technical problems of philosophy rather than of some other science solely by the fact that the primitives out of which that persistent attempt generates them are the philosophical primitives, viz., appraisals such as described.

6. *Is All Philosophy Ultimately Concerned with Appraisals?*—

It would generally be granted that the questions as to what are beauty and ugliness, right and wrong, truth and error, etc., are philosophical questions. But it would be claimed by many that the problems of metaphysics—problems concerning the nature and the form, structure, or order of reality— are among the most important of philosophical problems and yet are not either directly or indirectly about appraisals. Philosophy, that is to say, includes the "normative sciences," but cannot be equated to them because it also includes metaphysics, which is not one of them.

I believe that this claim concerning metaphysics is ill-founded, and that every "metaphysical" problem for which it is made either (*a*) is directly about some appraisal; or (*b*) is derivative from some appraisal (i.e., is indirectly about some appraisal); or (*c*) belongs to some science other than philosophy; or (*d*) rests on false assumptions and is therefore spurious; or (*e*) is a priori insoluble because the statement purporting to formulate it is so ambiguous that one cannot tell from it just what the problem is supposed to be—what the data of it are and what the *dubitatum* or *quaesitum*—or whether a problem is there at all, or rather only a string of individually meaningful words followed by a question mark.

As regards the last sort of case in particular, I submit that, in a large part of what has gone by the name of metaphysics, the meaning of the terms employed has been left so vague and the transitions of thought so loose that the conclusions drawn have no title whatever to the name of knowledge, even of probabilities. "Metaphysics" or "philosophy" of this kind therefore seems to me to be just what Broad calls it, namely, moonshine. It is not really philosophy but only the manifestation of a methodological naïveté, if not disease, from which philosophy is gradually freeing itself. But the need to purge of it the philosophical problems it has infected does not imply, as logical positivists have claimed, that all the problems of metaphysics vanish in the attempt to state them clearly and are therefore pseudo-problems. I believe on the contrary that some of them are genuine, and that the reformulation that frees the statement of them from ambiguities and false assumptions makes solution of them possible at least in principle.

This is true in particular of the problem of the nature of reality. What this problem actually is has, I believe, been widely misconceived. The adjectives "real" and "unreal," as they enter into the statement of a metaphysical position, do not designate any character that any things have independently of human interest in them, but are on the contrary adjectives of human appraisal. The adjective real voices appraisal of something as being of a species which is of interest at the time to the person applying the adjective; and the adjective unreal, on the contrary, voices appraisal of something as belonging to a species of no interest to him at the time and therefore as to be ignored by him. This implies that a general statement as to the nature of reality, that is, a statement of the form "to be real is to be such and such," does not formulate a hypothesis and is therefore not susceptible of being proved, disproved, or assigned a probability. Rather, it formulates simply the criterion of interestingness which we use or propose to use at a given time in appraising any given thing as interesting or uninteresting to us.

To be using, or to choose, such a criterion is to be occupying, or to take, an ontological position. Since an ontological position is thus not a hypothesis but a (for the time) ruling interest, an ontological position is not the sort of thing susceptible of being either erroneous or the opposite. An ontological position may be queer and unusual, or on the contrary widely held; or it may be perhaps foolish or wise in the long run; or it may be taken, given up, or not taken; or it may be stated or not stated; but it may not be either refuted, demonstrated, or shown to be less or more probable than another. These categories simply do not apply to the sort of thing an ontological position is. For example, as already pointed out, the ontological position of the natural scientist is that to be real—that is, to be of interest to him in his capacity as natural scientist—is to be either perceptually public or implicit in what is so. To take this position is obviously not to contend anything, but to adopt a criterion of interestingness—the one which defines both the scope and the limits of "natural science." But since nothing is contended by adopting it, there is nothing there to be proved or refuted. Adoption of it can only be either imitated or not imitated. [4]

From these considerations it follows that the problem of ontology is at least misleadingly stated by the question, "What is the nature of reality?" For this form of statement suggests that the problem is logically analogous to, for instance, the problem, "What is the nature of rubber, or of a seed, etc.?" in which some entity, called "rubber" or "a seed," etc., is concretely given to us, whose properties we are then asked to discover. The problem of ontology is not of this kind. It is better described as that of inquiring, as we have just done, what exactly it is we are saying about any-thing—e.g., about matter, or about mind, or about whatever is perceived, etc.—when we deny or assert that it is real or ask whether it is real; and further, of inquiring what principal varieties there may be of such ontological choices, how they are mutually related, what is demanded by con-sistency with any given one of them, etc.

---

[4] Perception of this is what dictates the "ontological liberalism" described by the writer in "A Defense of Ontological Liberalism," *Jour. of Phil.*, XXI, No. 13 (June, 1924).

There are certain other problems also often regarded as belonging to metaphysics, but described as cosmological rather than ontological. Examples would be the problem of the nature of the causal relation and its kinds; that of the relation between mind and body; that of the origin of mind, etc. A word must be said to indicate how such problems would be classified on the hypothesis I have presented as to the subject matter of philosophy.

The problems connected with the causal relation are derivative problems of the theory of knowledge. They are raised automatically by any attempt to give a thoroughgoing account of the difference between knowledge and error, and of the kinds of knowledge. The problem of the relation between causation and teleology is likewise a derivative problem belonging to the theory of knowledge. On the other hand, the question whether the events of nature, or any given one of them is determined teleologically or on the contrary in "blindly" causal manner is not a philosophical one. Rather, it is philosophical only in so far as the doubt concerns the meaning of the question—the nature of causation, of teleology, of determinism. For obviously if a man who was working on a roof fell off, the question whether it was an accident, mechanically caused perhaps by the fact that his foot slipped, or, on the contrary, suicide so planned that his wife could collect his life insurance, is not a philosophical question but one of historical fact, perhaps impossible to decide. Equally historical, of course, even if unanswerable by us, would be the question whether his fall was brought about by the purposive action of some god, demon, or other occult being.

The question of the origin of mind—once we know exactly what is to be understood by "mind"—is likewise historical, not philosophical. Again, the problem of the relation of mind to body is philosophical only in so far as it turns on how these terms are to be defined, which is a derivative question belonging to the theory of knowledge. But if this is assumed to be adequately known already, and a problem still remains—turning, let us say, on whether a given mental event is strictly simultaneous with or, on the contrary, immediately sequent to a certain neural event in the brain cortex—then the problem is once more not philosophical. Rather it is chronological, and soluble, if at all, only on the basis of accurate timing of the two events.

That all the problems of metaphysics are directly or indirectly about appraisals could be shown only by examining all the problems which have been called metaphysical, and showing in the case of each which of the alternatives (*a* to *e* above) actually fits it. This would take a volume in itself, but perhaps the few examples just discussed will suffice to show why these problems do not seem to me to constitute cases invalidating my contention as to the subject matter distinctive of philosophy.

7. *Philosophy, the Branches of Philosophy, and the Philosophies of Particular Subjects.*—A predicate taken in a given sense is predicable without incongruity, whether affirmatively, negatively, or interrogatively, only of the entities of a certain class, which may be a broad or narrow one and more or less clearly marked off. For example, it is only of physical substances that one can without incongruity question whether, or affirm or deny that, they are soluble in alcohol. It is only of persons who have attempted something that one can congruously ask whether, or deny or affirm that, they have succeeded.[5] These remarks apply to predicates of appraisal as

---

[5] It might be thought that one could congruously and truly deny of George Washington that he succeeded in jumping Niagara Falls: he never attempted it; therefore he cannot have succeeded; therefore he did not. This, however, overlooks

to any others. For instance, the adjective "erroneous" is congruously predicable only of opinions; the adjective "formally fallacious" only of inferences; the adjective "veracious" only of statements or of the persons who make them; the adjective "morally wrong" only of the conduct of responsible beings, etc. An exhaustive analysis of the nature of the characters predicated respectively by these adjectives and their opposites, together with an account of the relations to one another of the sorts of entities constituting the realm of congruous predicability of each, is what the philosophy of opinions, the philosophy of inferences, the philosophy of statements, etc., consists of.[6]

But these three philosophies, for example, are not mutually independent but on the contrary connected indissolubly with one another, and together (with certain other parts) comprise the philosophy of knowledge. When "philosophy" or "the branches of philosophy" are mentioned in ordinary discourse, what is referred to is the philosophy of such comprehensive subjects as knowledge, conduct, religion, art, aesthetic experience, etc.

---

the fact that congruous denial consists in assertion of an opposite, and that "he did not succeed" is not opposite of "he succeeded" unless taken in the sense of "he failed" and not in the sense of "he either failed, or studied medicine, or became president, or was born in America, etc." (that is, not in the sense that "some predicate[s] simply other than 'having succeeded' is[are] predicable of him"). For if the assertion "he did not succeed" means that he failed, then what it means is false. If on the other hand what the assertion means is true, then it does not mean that he failed but that he neither succeeded nor failed; and this is not congruous denial of "he succeeded," since it is not assertion of an opposite of this, but (by implication) of the opposite of "he tried." The assertion "Washington did not succeed in jumping the Falls" is thus incongruous—impertinent—in exactly the same sense as the question "Have you quit beating your mother?" which is often used in textbooks on logic to illustrate the fallacy of "double question" (better described as fallacy of false insinuation, since assertion or denial involves this as much as question).

[6] On the other hand, the predicate "soluble in alcohol" is not a predicate of appraisal, and therefore a theory of the nature of solubility in alcohol would not be a philosophical theory but a physical one.

But any of these branches, or for instance again the philosophy of knowledge, is susceptible not only of division into parts (dealing specifically with inferences, opinions, etc.) but also of particularization in respect to what, specifically, the knowledge considered is knowledge of—for example, physical entities, mathematical entities, etc. Such particularization will give us the philosophy of physical knowledge, of mathematical knowledge, etc. But we could particularize further still, calling neither for the philosophy of knowledge in general, nor that of knowledge concerning the entities of physics in general, but perhaps only for that of knowledge concerning the entities of acoustics.[7] Then the account of, for instance, what "erroneousness" in the case of opinions about sound consists in would be framed in terms of kinds of tests too special to constitute also an account of what erroneousness consists in where an opinion specifically about light, for example, is concerned instead. Or, to turn from the philosophy of knowledge to the philosophy of conduct, we might be interested not in the philosophy of conduct in general, but only, for instance, in that of the conduct of physicians, or of tennis players, etc., as such; that is, in the ethics of medical practice, of games in general or, more specifically, of tennis playing, etc.

These examples illustrate what is meant by the philosophy of this or that particular subject as distinguished from philosophy in general, or from the comprehensive branches of philosophy.

8. *Is Philosophy Mere "Rationalization" of Our Appraisals?*—
The situations which naturally generate philosophical theorizing in rational persons have been described above as those

---

[7] The theory of sound is not philosophical theory, but the theory of our knowledge of sound is philosophical.

in which challenge of their appraisals occurs—the philosophizing consisting essentially in the attempt to find major premises from which can be logically deduced the appraisals challenged as well as others that are on the contrary accepted. The question now presents itself whether philosophizing is not then only what is called "rationalizing"—the inventing of reasons adequate to support opinions we already hold, so that the opinions determine the reasons instead of the reasons the opinions.

But to raise this question is, by implication, equally to raise the question whether the theorizing engaged in by, for instance, the physicist, is not similarly rationalizing. For he too starts from opinions he already has—propositions already accepted by him as being laws of nature—and attempts to find premises from which they can be deduced. In the case of the philosopher, the facts the theory is cut to fit consist of generalizations of particular appraisals actually made by certain human beings. In that of the physicist, they consist of generalizations of particular facts of nature, which are independent of man's appraisal. This is what differentiates the theorizing as in the first case philosophical and in the second physical. But the theorizing enterprise (as distinguished from its subject matter) is exactly the same sort of enterprise in both cases. Therefore, if it is "mere rationalization" in philosophy, it is equally so in physics; or, if it is not so in physics, then it is not so, or at least need not be so, in philosophy either. In the chapter following, I propose to consider more carefully than I have done up to this point what a theory is, what its functions are, and the criteria for choice between rival theories. It will appear that beside a certain likeness there is also a great difference—equally in philosophy and in physics—between theory construction (which is an epistemically fruitful process) and mere rationalization (which is an epistemically barren one). It is the difference between speculation when disciplined by the requirement that it meet certain objective tests of validity, and speculation when on the contrary irresponsible because uncontrolled or insufficiently controlled by such tests. That a great deal of philosophical speculation has actually been of this irresponsible sort, and in consequence barren of genuine knowledge, does not at all imply that philosophical speculation cannot be as rigorously controlled as is physical speculation, and as truly fruitful.

CHAPTER ELEVEN

The Empirical and the Theoretical
Tasks of Any Scientific Inquiry

IN THE development of any scientific inquiry—it makes no
difference what its subject matter may be—experience and
reason play parts equally indispensable. To torture the word
"experience" in such manner as will pack into its meaning
the part of reason, or to do conversely, is a futile procedure
whose only fruit could be to save the mere label "empiricism"
or "rationalism" for use as an epistemological battle cry.
But discernment of the roles of experience and reason in
knowledge eliminates the *casus belli* itself and therefore also
the need for battle cries.

   1. *Experience and Reason.*—A science begins by attempting
to discover laws—regularities—among its primitive facts.
Certain of these facts are observed to resemble one another in
certain respects, and these mutually resemblant facts are
sometimes observed to be regularly correlated with certain
other facts also resembling one another in certain respects.
The outcome of such observations is the conceiving of kinds
(of which various primitive facts or their elements are cases),
and the detecting of the empirical laws we commonly call the
properties of things.[1] These laws are more or less venturesome

---

[1] Failure to distinguish between *qualities* and *properties* breeds endless difficulties. For

generalizations of the regularities that were found among the facts observed: we venture to believe that they are present also among the unobserved or not yet observed facts of the same kinds.

Even when additional observations confirm the validity of the generalizations, however, the scientific mind is not satisfied. It insists on asking not only what laws there are but also why they are what in particular they are; what the exact scope of each is; and whether or how they are connected with one another. It seeks not only knowledge but also understanding of the laws of the field it studies. But demand for explanation of a law empirically discovered is not met by subsumption of it under another more general empirical law. That wax melts when subjected to heat is not explained by mention of the fact that all solids do so under the influence of heat. Explanation of an empirical law is provided only by theory—by a theory of the sort of fact which the law merely asserts. And the construction of theory is that part of the development of a body of knowledge in which the requirements of reason dictate most completely and obviously. It is, however, already at their behest that we insist on generalizing our observations—on postulating that the regularities we

---

this reason, it is important to bear in mind that a property is the sort of attribute that always has the form of a law. Thus in the case of properties of the entities of nature, to say that entity O has property P is to say that O is such that if a change of kind A occurs in environment of kind E of O, a change of kind B regularly occurs in O. Cf. Emile Meyerson, *Identité et réalité*, pp. 33 f. Or in some cases, to say that O has property P is to say that O is such that whenever O has property Q it has also property R (and sometimes also that whenever it has R it has Q.) In the case of a mathematical entity, e.g., the number 17, to say that it has the property of being "prime" is to say that it is such that if the arithmetical operation called division is performed upon 17 then the remainder is 0 when and only when the divisor is either 17 or 1. Opinions, beliefs, dispositions, habits, are similarly properties of the minds that have them, in the sense of being laws of these minds: being Republican is a property of the mind of Herbert Hoover in exactly the same sense of "property" as that in which being malleable is a property of certain pieces of steel. Cf. the writer's "On the Attributes of Material Things," *Jour. of Phil.*, XXXI, No. 3 (Feb., 1934).

have experienced are not limited to the particular set of cases in which we have actually experienced them.

Theory, however, is not independent of and, still less, opposable to experience, for the theorizing is about the very laws that observation and experiment have discovered. Moreover, as theory develops, laws hitherto unsuspected are deduced from it, and experience comes gradually to function not so much as a source of material for inductive generalizations, but more and more rather as a test of the validity in experience of laws obtained deductively from theory about certain experienced facts.

This broad sketch of the roles of observation or experience and of reason in the development of scientific knowledge in general is applicable not only to the natural sciences but also to mathematics. E. Goblot[2] points out that

It is through trials that Pythagoras seems to have discovered the curious properties of certain numbers and of certain series of numbers. In this way he found that the sum of consecutive odd numbers is always a perfect square. The sums of consecutive whole numbers and the sums of even numbers also have general properties. Nowadays we should write them as follows:

$$1 + 2 + 3 + \ldots + n = \frac{n(n+1)}{2}$$
$$1 + 3 + 5 + \ldots + 2n\text{-}1 = n^2$$
$$2 + 4 + 6 + \ldots + 2n = n(n+1)$$

It is one thing, however, to discover empirically such properties of certain numbers, and to confirm more and more, by means of more and more extensive observations of particular numbers of the same kind; the generalization which extends these properties to all numbers of that kind; and it is another thing to prove, deductively, that the properties necessarily hold of all numbers of the given kind. The attempt to provide

---

[2] *Essai sur la classification des sciences* (1898), chap. ii, p. 27.

deductive proof of them, or of other mathematical propositions already for one reason or another regarded as probably
true, and to deduce new ones from the same premises, is the
sort of task that engages most of the attention of mathematicians.

In the natural sciences, on the other hand, especially in
those in which theory is not yet greatly advanced, the task
of discovering valid empirical generalizations looms much
larger than it does in mathematics. But both sorts of tasks
are present in each case. The fundamental difference between
the natural sciences and mathematics is not that the method
of the former is exclusively empirical and that of the latter
exclusively deductive, but that the entities whose properties
the natural scientist investigates experimentally are entities
merely presented to him by perception, whereas those whose
properties the mathematician investigates (also experimentally) are entities created by his own verbal stipulations. The
operations to be performed in experimental investigation of
the former accordingly are physical operations; in the case of
the latter, they are arithmetical or other mathematical operations. But in both cases alike there remains the difference
between simply finding, after performance, that a certain
operation upon certain entities does have a certain outcome,
and proving, independently of such performance, that it must
have that very outcome. It is therefore not from difference
in this respect that the contrast arises between the probability
of natural laws and the necessity of mathematical theorems.
It arises on the contrary from the fact that in mathematics
all the properties of the entities to be studied are implicitly
fixed by the stipulations which created these entities, whereas
in natural science the properties of the entities to be studied
are not fixed by perceptual observation, since perception does
not create but only discloses these entities.

The statements of the defining properties of mathematical entities thus are stipulations, not hypotheses, and their defining properties are therefore known with certainty to start with. But the statements of the defining properties of natural entities always remain hypotheses only, and their defining properties (viz., those from which all their remaining ones can be inferred) are therefore not known to start with but only to end with, and then not with certainty but only with a degree of probability always short of the highest.

In philosophy, observation and theory—experience and reason—likewise both enter, and the role of each there is of essentially the same nature as in all other knowledge-seeking enterprises. To show that this is indeed the case, we need first to consider more carefully what exactly theory is in general, and what function it performs, and then to point out of what sort the empirical generalizations of philosophy are, and how the validity of any theory which philosophy constructs to explain or demonstrate them is to be empirically tested. To the first of these two tasks the remaining sections of the present chapter are devoted.

2. *Theory, Conjecture, and Law.*—It is sometimes said that a theory is the sort of thing which, when it has received enough confirmation, acquires the status of a law. Theory in this sense of the word would be synonymous with conjectural law. For example, one notices that various pieces of wax have been exposed to heat and that they have melted. One then may form the theory, that is, the conjecture, that when wax is exposed to heat it always melts. This is a conjecture concerning a law of the behavior of wax, i.e., concerning a property of wax, and if experimental investigation confirms it, we then describe the proposition no longer as a theory or conjecture but as a now known law of the behavior of wax.

Theory in the sense of conjecture, however, has no special connection with laws, for there are conjectures that concern not laws but particular facts. An example would be the theory or conjecture that Bacon and not Shakespeare wrote *Hamlet*. It is obvious that if ever this theory should be proved, the proposition that Bacon wrote *Hamlet* would not thereupon become describable as a law; for a law is a proposition concerning any case of a given kind, not concerning one particular fact, whether conjectural or established. But although some theories (in the sense merely of conjectures) are thus not conjectural laws, the theories which are about laws—whether in the sense of being conjectural laws, or in another sense to be described later—are always at least conjectures, since otherwise we should call what they assert not theory but known fact.

3. *Theory as Explanatory Conjecture.*—"Theory," however, seldom means simply conjecture (whether in respect to law or particular fact). Usually it means at least explanatory conjecture; and when scientific theories are mentioned, such as Fourier's theory of heat conduction or the dynamic theory of gases, then theory means in addition conjecture explanatory of laws. But before inquiring into the difference between the sorts of conjectures explanatory of, respectively, laws and particular facts, we must first be clear as to what explanation, no matter of what, essentially consists in.

It is sometimes said that science does not explain but only describes—that it does not tell us why things happen as they do, but only how they happen. But obviously this is not true unless, to begin with, we force upon the question "Why?" some mystical or foolish meaning not intended by those who, day in and day out, ask it and get it satisfactorily answered. I recently had occasion to ask, for instance, why my oil-burning furnace failed to start when the thermostat called for heat, and my question was eventually answered by the statement that it was because the contact points in the electrical relay had become corroded, and whenever this occurs the electric current no longer passes through. This was exactly the sort of information that my demand for an explanation, through the question "Why?" was meant to elicit. To say that even if that information was true it did not constitute explanation would be simply to refuse to use the word "explanation" in the sense it has in ordinary English, and to force upon it instead, *ad damnandum*, some unusual one. Again, the particular fact that a given piece of wax has melted can be explained, for instance, by supposing that the sun has been shining upon it, and recalling that exposure of wax to heat regularly causes it to melt. The law also, that exposure of wax to heat regularly causes it to melt, can be explained, although the explanation of it would be more esoteric. Without attempting to give it here, we can say that it would consist of a statement that the structure of wax is molecular, and of a description of heat and of melting in terms of molecular behavior.

We may be told, however, that when the explanations offered in these or any other cases are examined, they are found to consist only of descriptions of the *explicandum* in more general terms. But to say this is obviously to abandon the claim that science does not explain but only describes, and to substitute for it the admission that science does explain, together with the claim that explanation consists of description in more general terms. Even this claim, however, is hardly admissible. To explain the fact that a given piece of wax melted by saying that it was exposed to heat is not to describe in more general terms its having melted; it is to assert the antecedent occurrence of a particular event of another kind, already known to be capable of causing wax to

melt. Again, to explain in terms of molecular changes the law
that exposure of wax to heat regularly causes it to melt, is to
define and postulate a respect of identity between being heated
and melting, and to do this could only very elliptically be
called describing that law in more general terms.

The essential nature of explanation is much rather that,
given an *explicandum* Q, an explanation of it always has the
form: Because P, and if P, then Q. That is, the *explicans* of a
given *explicandum* always consists of the major and minor
premises of some hypothetical syllogism in the *modus ponens*,
having the *explicandum* as conclusion.[3]

4. *No Conjecture Really Explanatory if It Lacks "Predictiveness."*—To be really and not only apparently explanatory, however, a conjecture must imply some facts additional to the
facts (particular or general) which it was devised to explain,
for otherwise the *implicans* and the implicate are exactly
equipollent, and what is offered as explanation is only a
disguised assertion that there is some explanation, plus a
mere name by which to refer to that still unknown explanation. And obviously, to give a name to what one is ignorant
of does not in the least replace the ignorance by knowledge.
Examples of such pseudo-explanation would be that a watch
ticks because there is a "ticker" in it, that material objects
attract one another because of "gravitation," or that opium
makes people sleep because of its "soporific power." The requirement that, if a conjecture is to be really explanatory, it
must imply something additional to the *explicandum*, may be
stated otherwise by saying that the conjecture must have

---

[3] The major premise of the hypothetical syllogism must consist of some law of
connection, whether causal or conceptual. That is, no basis for explanation is provided
by a law of mere joint incidence. For example, that giraffes have cloven hoofs is not
explained by the fact that giraffes are ruminants and the conjecture that all ruminants
have cloven hoofs.

some predictive capacity. The question whether the predictions it makes turn out to be true or false is another matter, which determines not whether it is explanatory in kind, but whether the particular explanation it advances is a tenable or untenable one.

The requirement of predictive capacity holds whether the *explicandum* be a particular fact or a general fact (a law). But predictiveness, in the sense which the word has here, may be equally of past, present, or future events, or of known as well as of yet unknown laws. For to speak of a conjecture as predictive of a fact F means only that F was not one of the facts the conjecture was devised to explain; that, so far as could be seen independently of the conjecture, F was unconnected with these facts; and that F can be deduced from the conjecture.

5. *Theory as Conceptually (vs. Causally) Explanatory Conjecture.*—The next thing to consider is the important difference between conjectures explanatory of laws and conjectures explanatory of particular events. The latter are conjectures as to some other particular event. For example, the particular event that this wax has melted is tentatively explained by the conjecture that the wax was exposed to heat, and by mention of the empirically known law that exposure of wax to heat causes it to melt. But a law, for instance the one just mentioned, is not an event, and since only an event, viz., a change or a "non-change," can strictly speaking be a cause or an effect, the conjecture explanatory of a law cannot, as with an event, be that a certain event occurred, which stood to that law as cause to effect.[4] Rather, what explains a law is

---

[4] The two notions of "cause" and "agent" are often not discriminated. For instance, we say loosely that a given person caused a certain accident, but strictly speaking it was an act or a volition of that person, i.e., an event, which, under the circum-

always something standing to it in the relation of conceptual *implicans* to implicate; and a theory, in the sense we are essentially concerned with here, is always something standing in that relation to what it explains. The nature of that relation may be clarified as follows.

If we take as *explicandum* not a law but a particular event, e.g., that this wax has melted, what we offer as explanation of it, e.g., that exposure to heat regularly causes wax to melt and that this wax was exposed to heat, does imply the *explicandum*, but in such a case the implication is not conceptual (rational, theoretical) but causal (empirical); that is, it rests on a law (a property of wax) inductively discovered; and contradiction of it would be contradiction of a law of nature. In the cases where the *explicandum* is a law, on the other hand, the implication is conceptual in the sense that it rests on a tentative definition—a tentative stipulation as to what the sort of perceived phenomenon called by a certain name shall be conceived to consist in essentially; so that a contradiction of the tentative *explicans* would be contradiction in terms.[5] A definition, however, is always an equation—the expression of an identity—so that, as Meyerson has emphasized, to explain, in the sciences, is essentially to discover some way of *conceiving* as identical certain phenomena that are

---

stances existing at the time, caused the accident. An agent—a doer—is a being, a certain change in whom (or in which) causes a certain change in something else. If desire for the latter change was the cause of the change in the agent which itself caused the change in the other entity, then the agent is a purposive agent and the causation is teleological. Another use of the word "cause" is that of Meyerson. By "cause" he means the "sufficient reason" of a law, not the "sufficient reason" of an event. This usage, although deliberate, is unfortunate because it clashes with the sense in which the word is ordinarily used. But Meyerson would agree—indeed insist—that what explains a law (whether or not it be called the "cause" of the law) is not an event.

[5] Cf. Hume's distinction between denial of assertions as to matters of fact and of assertions as to relations of ideas (*Inquiry Concerning Human Understanding*, Part I, sec. iv) and Carnap's distinction between the P-rules and the L-rules of language (*P. L. S.*, pp. 50 f.).

perceived as different.[6] For instance, in the example of the wax, increase of temperature and liquefaction are both conceived as increase of molecular motion.[7]

6. *Structure of the Theories Explanatory of Laws.*—The question arises, however, as to how the invention of concepts, through prescriptive definitions, can imply a law of nature, which is a relation not between invented concepts but between kinds of natural events (our concepts of which, when we have any, are empirical, i.e., are not invented by us but dictated to us by inductive observation).

The answer is that a theory explanatory of empirical laws does not consist solely of a set of definitions and postulates creative of certain concepts, but includes also, and indispensably, a method for the identification of the empirical entities that are to be regarded as exemplifying (or as nearly enough exemplifying) those concepts. That is, the theory includes either a prescription that, or a prescription for deciding whether or not (for purposes of explanation and prediction of the given empirical laws), a given invented concept and a given empirical concept are to be treated as if they were

---

[6] Meyerson, *op. cit.* The principle of "causality," i.e., as he uses the term, the principle of explanation, "is but the principle of identity applied to the existence of objects in time" (p. 38), and "where we employ it, the phenomenon becomes rational, adequate to our reason: we understand it and are able to explain it" (p. 35). This statement of Meyerson's, however, applies only to explanation of laws. But there is also such a thing as explanation of particular events, and in their case explanation consists not in conceiving as in some way identical two things perceived as different, but in suggesting an adequate cause-event.

[7] In the case of a particular event it seems possible to ask both for a conceptual (rational, theoretical) and for a causal (empirical) explanation. To ask for the the latter is to ask what other particular event probably caused the given one. The particular event which was the cause explains no other particular event of the same kind. It therefore explains a strictly unique particular. But to ask for a conceptual explanation of a given particular event is to speak elliptically, for strictly it is to ask how any event of its kind (and therefore also itself) must be conceived in order to account for the laws of occurrence of events of that kind. And explanation in this sense is not explanation of, uniquely, the given particular event.

identical, i.e., the exemplifications of the latter regarded as exemplifications of the former.[8]

These two parts of any theory explanatory of laws—the definitions or other stipulations creative of concepts and the operation or method prescribed for deciding what empirical entities shall be regarded as exemplifying the created concepts—have been called by Norman Campbell respectively the "hypothesis" and the "dictionary" of the theory; by Bridgman (when the theory is mathematical) the "equations" and the "text"; and by more recent writers the "syntax" and the "semantics" of the theory. The second of these two parts is, I believe, what F. S. C. Northrop has in mind when he speaks of "epistemic correlations."[9]

7. *Grounds for Choice between Rival Theories.*—If the laws which one theory attempts to explain are incompatible with

---

[8] Cf. Kant's contention that the pure categories of the understanding are heterogeneous to empirical intuitions, and that, to render the former applicable to the latter, or the latter recognizable in the former, there must be available a third thing, homogeneous with both, viz., the "transcendental schema" of the understanding.

[9] Campbell, *op. cit.*, p. 122; Bridgman, *op. cit.*, p. 59; J. H. Woodger, *The Technique of Theory Construction*, p. 6. It is from Whewell, however, that the writer first gained the general idea of the structure of theories. Cf. in particular the following passage from the *Novum Organon Renovatum* (Bk. II, chap. ii, sec. ii, art. 7): "It is very important for us to observe that these controversies [about the right definition of certain terms in science] have never been questions of insulated and *arbitrary* definitions, as men seem often tempted to suppose them to have been. In all cases there is a tacit assumption of some Proposition which is to be expressed by means of the Definition, and which gives it its importance. The dispute concerning the Definition thus acquires a real value, and becomes a question concerning true and false."

Campbell points out that a theory cannot be said to explain a law merely if the the theory is such that the law can be deduced from it. In addition, he believes, the propositions of the "hypothesis" of the theory must display an analogy—be similar in form—to the laws the theory is to explain. But he does not specify how we can tell whether such analogy is present, or present in sufficient degree, or in relevant respects. And in the absence of specification of this, one may say that some analogy can, with sufficient ingenuity, always be exhibited. It seems to me that the only test of the relevance and sufficiency of any analogy exhibited by the "hypothesis" of a theory is whether the theory possesses predictive capacity in the sense already stated, and therefore that if this requirement is satisfied, that of analogy is superfluous.

those which another theory attempts to explain, what we then have is a conflict of data rather than of theories; and the task we immediately confront is not to decide which theory is the better, but which data are erroneous. If, however, the laws which two theories attempt to explain are the same, then the questions in the light of which one of the theories is to be preferred to the other are as follows:

a) Whether one but not the other implies all the laws that were to be explained;

b) Whether, if both do, one but not the other has predictive capacity, i.e., implies some laws additional to those that were to be explained;

c) Whether, if both have predictive capacity and any of their predictions conflict, observation verifies the predictions of one but confutes some prediction of the other;

d) Whether, if observation bears out the predictions of both, one predicts everything the other predicts, but something more also;

e) Whether, if both are equal in the foregoing respects so far as tested, one is psychologically simpler, i.e., more convenient to use than the other.

If one theory predicts certain laws that observation verifies and that the other theory is not able to predict, and conversely, then we are not called upon to choose between them but, for the time being, we use each for what it alone is able to do, and use either one indifferently for what both alike are able to do. But in such a case the desire for integration of our knowledge, which moves us to the construction of theories, is not satisfied until we succeed in devising some theory which predicts everything each of the others separately predicts.

8. *The Facts Which a Given Theory Seeks to Explain Often De-*

rivative.—In the preceding discussion, the laws which a theory attempts to explain and predict have been described as empirical laws, obtained inductively from examination of some of the primitive facts of the given field of inquiry. It should be clear, however, that the laws to be explained may in a given case be more or less remotely derivative from these instead of obtained thus directly from primitive facts. The structure of a theory—as in essence consisting of a definition of one or more terms predicated in the given laws and of a method for determining whether any given entity is or is not to be accepted as a case of the *definiens*—this structure, and likewise the explanatory and heuristic powers it possesses if it meets the tests of validity described, remain the same no matter how the laws given as *explicanda* in a particular case may have been obtained.

Moreover, in view of the tendency already pointed out that derivative facts will bulk larger than primitives in the picture of an inquiry as it develops, we may expect the laws with which most of the theories in a given field concern themselves to be more or less remote derivatives of that field; and in the statements of these, no explicit mention of the primitives will occur. This will be true in philosophy as well as in other sciences, and will mean that although appraisals are the primitive facts of philosophy, the majority of the terms for which philosophy has to seek valid definitions will not be terms of appraisal. They will be terms standing not for primitive philosophical facts but for facts which are philosophical only because implicit in the philosophical primitives.

When the facts—whether philosophical or other—which a theory attempts to explain are not laws directly obtained by induction from the primitives of the given field, but are derivatives from these, they can be described as empirical only in the sense that, no matter how abstract they are, their factuality has nevertheless indirectly been put to empirical test. Accordingly, the contrast between a theory and what it is about is better described as one between *quaesitum explicans* and *data explicanda* than as one between reason or theory on the one hand, and observation or experience on the other. As Whewell has pointed out, once we have accepted a theory, we describe our observations in terms of the concepts of it as a matter of course; and yesterday's successful theories thus tacitly permeate today's descriptions of empirical facts.[10]

---

[10] See, e.g., *Nov. Org. Renov.*, Bk. II, chap. v, sec. i, art. 4. In general, Whewell's account of scientific method anticipated modern views of the subject much more closely than did J. S. Mill's, which overshadowed Whewell's in its time.

CHAPTER TWELVE

Philosophical Experience and
Philosophical Theory

ADMITTEDLY, there has been no dearth of theorizing in philosophy, but too often the theories have been presented as
if they were revelations from God to philosophers rather than
speculations to be tested. In consequence, philosophical
theorizing has been largely barren of the fruits that speculation, recognized as such and accordingly subjected to appropriate controls, has proved itself capable of yielding in other
fields. This state of affairs, I believe, is chiefly owing to the
fact that philosophical theorizing has in the vast majority
of cases been carried on with little or no clear consciousness
of the structure of explanatory theories in general, or of the
empirical generalizations that philosophical theory has to
explain, or of the nature of the primitive facts by reference to
which the validity of philosophical theories is to be tested,
or of the sorts of empirical tests the theories must meet.

Part II of the present work seeks to clarify these very questions, and it is for this reason that the attempt has been made
(chap. x) to point out the sort of facts that are primitive
for philosophy, and (chap. xi) to describe the general nature
of explanatory theories and of their data, and the criteria for
choice between rival theories. In the present chapter, the
attempt will be made to elucidate the questions remaining

for consideration among these, and to make evident as a result that theorizing has in philosophy the same nature and functions as elsewhere, and that its validity is here also susceptible of being empirically tested.

1. *Approach to the Problem of Theory through the Example of Ethics.*—For the sake of the lucidity that goes with concrete examples, the discussion will be worded first in terms of the field of ethics. It will not, however, present any particular ethical theory, but only a theory as to the nature of ethical theory in general—that is, to use a terminology now becoming familiar, an ethical metatheory. Afterwards the considerations adduced will be shown to apply also, *mutatis mutandis*, to the other branches of philosophy and therefore to define a theory of the nature and method of philosophy in general—that is, a philosophical metatheory.

2. *What Facts Are Primitive for Ethics?*—The facts primitive for a given science, we have already seen, are the sort of facts about which (directly or indirectly) are all the questions asked by the science, and by appeal to which also the theories constructed by the science are finally tested empirically. The facts primitive in this sense for philosophy, it was contended, consist of certain appraisals. It is now submitted that the facts primitive in the same sense specifically for ethics consist of some of the appraisals that would be expressed by such statements as: "This act is wrong"; "This man is evil"; "This ought to be done"; "This state of affairs is good," etc. These are appraisals of particulars and are all, no matter what their particular form, appraisals of the kinds called approval or disapproval. Those among them which constitute the primitive facts for ethics are the spontaneous or empirical ones, in the sense of these terms already stated—that is, the

ones which are not deduced from some ethical theory which the judging person was taught or constructed for himself, and which are not simply an imitation of other persons' approvals and disapprovals.

That some approvals and disapprovals are spontaneous in this sense is shown by the obvious fact that, for instance, neither teaching nor the holding of any ethical theory is needed by a mother to disapprove of an attempt to harm her infant, or by a man to disapprove of his house being set on fire or to approve of being helped to put out the fire, or indeed by a dog to disapprove of another dog's attempt to take his bone away from him. Moreover, unless some approvals and disapprovals were spontaneous in the sense stated, no categorical but only hypothetical approvals or disapprovals could even be derivative.

3. *Empirical Ethical Generalizations and Ethical Norms.*—By comparing the concretely given individual subjects of certain sets of spontaneous approvals or disapprovals, it is possible to arrive inductively at certain ethical generalizations, which are therefore also spontaneous or empirical in the sense of being neither derived from any ethical theory nor borrowed from other persons. For example, a number of acts, each of which we spontaneously disapprove, may resemble one another in being all of them cases of our having had the fruits of our labor taken from us without our consent. We may conclude inductively with the empirical ethical generalization that we disapprove of any act of this kind—a kind commonly called, perhaps, stealing or robbery or exploitation. The verbal expression of this generalized disapproval would be some such statement as "stealing from us is wrong," or perhaps, more sweepingly, "stealing is wrong." Empirical generalizations such as this are the analogues, in the field of

ethics, of such empirical generalizations in the field of natural science, as that heat causes wax to melt, or that glass is brittle, etc.

Maxims such as "stealing from me is wrong," "stealing from anyone is wrong," etc., are ethical norms. If they are arrived at in the way just described—directly by induction from spontaneous disapprovals or approvals—they are empirical ethical norms. Ethical norms, however, are in some cases arrived at deductively from some ethical theory the validity of which has already been well tested. They are then rational (i.e., theoretically grounded) ethical norms.

4. *What an Ethical Theory Explains and Predicts.*—Approvals and disapprovals are always somebody's approvals and disapprovals, but what an ethical theory attempts is not to point out what past events in a person's life are responsible for the fact that he now approves and disapproves what he does, nor to state what sorts of training, if he were subjected to them, would cause him to approve or disapprove something else. An inquiry of this sort—into the genesis of an individual's present approvals and disapprovals or into the laws of such genesis—would belong not to ethics but to the psychology of learning.

Again, ethical theorizing, like physical, does not attempt to show that the generalizations it concerns are valid—for in either case this is assumed already on the basis of inductions from particulars—but only to show why they are valid and exactly how far their scope extends. This is done by discovering premises from which these empirically discovered generalizations could have been deduced, and from which others empirically confirmable can be deduced.[1]

---

[1] That this is the task of ethical theory has been pointed out by J. Rueff in his book, *From the Physical to the Social Sciences* (1929), which deserves to be better known than

What we must now specially notice, however—for if we do not, hopeless confusion ensues—is that the problem it is attempted to solve by a theory of, for instance, right and wrong, is never, "What do the words right and wrong, considered as it were *in vacuo*, mean?" (for, simply by a verbal convention, they can be made to mean anything one chooses) but always, "What do these words mean, that is, imply, as applied to this, that, and that, or as applied to all cases of kinds K, L, M by person P or by persons P, Q, R?" For only then is the question as to what the words right and wrong mean not one of arbitrary definition but of real definition—that is, of what the words mean as *actually* applied by person P, in contrast with what he may propose to mean or think he means by them. This point is of cardinal importance not only here but for philosophical method in general, and will be considered subsequently in greater detail (chap. xiv).

It is then obvious that the implication of a term of approval or disapproval as spontaneously applied, e.g., of the term wrong, can be investigated—or a theory as to its implication tested empirically—only if we specify some of the particular facts or classes of facts to which the term is spontaneously applied, for the validity or invalidity of a theory of the nature of wrongness is always strictly relative to the spontaneous applications of the term which are to be explained. But, as we shall see before long, we must specify not only which applications of the term the theory attempts to explain, but also whose spontaneous applications they are —whether those of a given person, or those on which all the persons of a given group agree, or those on which everybody

---

it seems to be. The task of ethical theory, he contends, is to "enunciate a system of initial propositions, axioms, and definitions which, when fed into the reasoning machine, will produce theorems coinciding with the rules of practical morals" (p. 79).

agrees. The need for this is usually overlooked, with confusion of issues as a result.

5. *The Two Parts of an Ethical Theory and the Empirical Tests of Its Validity.*—Reduced to essentials, ethical theorizing, like physical or any other, consists in attempting, on the one hand, to invent a definition of the predicate of the generalizations to be explained, and on the other to specify a method for determining whether or not a given concrete case or class of cases is to be accepted as meeting the definition—the definition and method together satisfying certain requirements soon to be described. In the physical example of wax, the generalization was that wax has the property of melting when heated, and the predicates to be defined were "heated" and "melting." In the case of an ethical theory, the generalizations concerned might be, for instance, that killing, adultery, and stealing are wrong. Let us note, however, that if, as we are assuming, these generalizations formulate inductions from a number of spontaneous disapprovals by a given person or group of persons, then these generalizations state properties of the person (or persons) P. That is, they are inductions that person P is such that whenever he perceives or imagines killing, adultery, or stealing, he disapproves it (the word wrong being used to state the disapproval).

The definition sought of the predicate wrong is then one satisfying, first, the requirement that if its *definiens* D is substituted for that predicate in the given empirical generalizations, the resulting statements will be true. That is, if the proposed definition of wrong is that to be wrong is to have character D, this definition must be such that killing, adultery, and stealing do have character D. To determine whether or not they do have it, we have to apply the method (accompanying the proposed definition) for determining whether or not character D is present in a given case or class of cases. The statement of the method will have the general form: A given case (or any case of a given kind) shall be admitted as having character D if and only if, when it is subjected to a test of kind T, the outcome of the test is perceived to be O. Specification of such a test is necessary because the cases in which theorizing (instead of direct observation) has to be resorted to are those in which the subjects of the several generalizations present themselves to perception as heterogeneous; that is, a respect of homogeneity D in such cases can perhaps be conceived but not directly perceived.

For example, the *definiens* of wrong proposed might be "forbidden by God"; and it is not ascertainable by direct perceptual observation of cases of killing, adultery, or stealing, whether or not these modes of action are forbidden by God. The proposed definition of wrong therefore has to be coupled with specification of a method by which to ascertain this indirectly. Such a method might be, "consult the Bible." Then the first of the empirical tests of adequacy of the theory (of the meaning of wrong as spontaneously applied by P), which that definition and this method together constitute, is that killing, adultery, and stealing, which were spontaneously disapproved by person P, should be found among modes of action described in the Bible as forbidden by God. If they are so found, the theory to this extent fits the facts for which it attempts to provide a conceptual explanation—the facts, namely, consisting of spontaneous disapproval by person P of the three kinds of action mentioned.

The second of the tests of adequacy of the theory is that the character D be not possessed by given modes of action that P spontaneously approves. That is, the facts for which the theory attempts to furnish a conceptual explanation are not only that P spontaneously disapproves modes of conduct

A, B, C, but also that P spontaneously approves modes of conduct E, F, G.

But the theory must in addition, like explanatory theories anywhere else, meet the requirement of successful predictiveness, this comprising the third and fourth empirical tests of its validity. Meeting this requirement will mean that modes of conduct H, I, J, which have character D, and modes of conduct K, L, M, which do not have character D—but approval or disapproval of which by P was not taken into consideration in the devising of D—will turn out to be also modes of conduct that P respectively disapproves and approves spontaneously.

As already stated, P may be a given person, or a given group of persons, or even possibly everybody. But unless specification is made as to *who* P is—that is, *whose* spontaneous disapprovals and approvals the statements "A, B, C are wrong" and "E, F, G are right" respectively express—the predictions implicit in any theory of these disapprovals and approvals remain a priori insusceptible of being either verified or confuted, because these predictions are of additional spontaneous approvals or disapprovals by the *same* persons. The theory therefore remains insusceptible also of comparison in respect to predictiveness with any supposedly rival theory. Two ethical theories are rivals only when each attempts to explain conceptually the same given set of approvals and disapprovals by the same person or persons.[2]

6. *Grounds for Choice between Rival Ethical Theories.*—Failure

---

[2] The theory that "wrong," when applied to the subjects to which a person (or group) P spontaneously applies it, means D is supported or invalidated by observing whether the predictions implicit in D turn out true or false, and not by the testimony of P as to what he means by wrong. For his testimony as to this could represent only what he thinks he means by D, that is, only what he believes to be the theory of wrongness which would accurately predict his spontaneous applications of the term wrong.

to specify—or indeed to realize the need of specifying—which disapprovals and approvals a given ethical theory attempts to explain conceptually, and equally whose disapprovals and approvals they are, is responsible for much of the disagreement to be found in the field of ethical theory; and much of the disagreement in other fields of philosophy has an analogous source. On the other hand, if these points—viz., what exactly the theories are about—are specified, one knows immediately whether the theories really are rivals or not.

The theories, moreover, then become amenable to empirical confirmation or confutation, as in other fields. If they are rivals, choice between them is possible on the same sorts of empirical grounds (described in chap. xi) as in the case of any other explanatory theories. Such real joining of issues as there has been in ethical theorizing has been owing to the fact that, as Rueff points out, the parties to the disputes have been—actually even if tacitly—pretty well agreed to begin with that certain modes of conduct were wrong and certain others right. The rules which describe these modes of conduct are, he writes, "the practical morals of the moment in which we live and for our particular group. . . . . They are the product of life."[3]

7. *Can Ethical Theory Resolve Conflicts between Ethical Judgments?*—The occasions that give rise to ethical theorizing are conflicts between two or more of the ethical judgments—the approvals or disapprovals—of one person; or between the ethical judgments of one person and those of another; or hesitation between approval and disapproval in a given case (this being describable as conflict between inclination to approve and to disapprove). When a rational, i.e., systematic solution of such conflicts is desired, theorizing is automati-

---

[3] *Op. cit.*, 75, 77.

cally resorted to. But since an ethical theory is a conceptual explanation of given spontaneous ethical judgments, and two really conflicting judgments cannot logically both be vindicated by the same theory, it seems impossible that theory construction should resolve the conflicts that give rise to it. Each party to the conflict will take his own ethical judgments as the ones to be fitted by the theory; and the result will be two theories instead of one, and two theories which will not be rivals in the sense described above. That is, they will not be rival explanations of the same judgments, but the rivalry will be between the judgments themselves.

The actual situation, however, is seldom as hopeless as these reflections would suggest. Beside the judgment concerning which the parties disagree, there will usually be many other ethical judgments in which they agree; and it will be possible to construct a theory adequate to explain given ones among these and to predict successfully the remainder of them. To resolve the remaining disagreement rationally will then consist in deciding it on the *same* theory already admitted by both parties as adequate to explain and predict all the ethical judgments in which both agree. That is, a solution is rational if the judgment it proposes is one logically coherent with—deducible from the same theory as—the remainder of one's own judgments; and the possibility of resolving conflicts of ethical judgments by means of appeal to ethical theory thus postulates desire in each party for such integration or coherence among his own judgments. If this is not present, no rational but only an arbitrary solution is possible. An example will make clear that rational solution of conflicts between ethical judgments, through ethical theorizing, is a familiar and working process.

Suppose for instance that a number of persons all spontaneously disapprove of killing, adultery, and stealing, but that some of them countenance lying and some disapprove it. Suppose this disagreement leads them to seek a theory adequate to explain the ethical judgments mentioned as to which they all agree. And suppose they eventually settle upon, as adequate to do so, a theory whose constituent "definition" and "method" are:

The *definition*, that any act of a given kind is spontaneously disapproved (the disapproval being formulated by calling the act wrong) means that acts of this kind generally bring about more human unhappiness than happiness; and, the *method* for deciding whether or not a given kind of act is "wrong" according to this definition, that the disagreeing parties shall inquire together into the probable effects of acts of the given kind, and then take a vote as to whether the unhappiness probably involved in these effects is or is not greater than the happiness.[4]

Suppose further that according to this theory, gambling and drunkenness also would be wrong; and that it turns out that gambling and drunkenness actually are disapproved spontaneously by all the persons in our example. The theory is thereby shown to be capable also of true predictions. So far

---

[4] This hedonistic theory of right and wrong is introduced here only for purposes of illustration, and its intrinsic merits are therefore a side issue. It may not be amiss to remark, however, that the "hedonic calculus" usually proposed as method for deciding whether a given sort of act is wrong (on the hedonistic definition of wrong) is a process not performable even in principle, to say nothing of at will. No way is known for measuring pleasures and displeasures either in the "fundamental" or the "derived" manner (see chapter on measurement in Campbell's *What Is Science?*). Even if we knew how to measure them, no psychological or physical summation and subtraction operations are known, the results of which would be predicted by arithmetical summation and subtraction of the figures obtained by measurements. (Cf. "Symbols, Signs, and Signals," *loc. cit.*, pp. 48–50). It should be noted that a "calculus of self-realizations" is, for similar reasons, likewise *flatus vocis*. On the other hand, the method specified in the text above, even if not as neat as one could wish, is practicable, and is approximately the one actually used when decisions have to be reached as to whether less, or more, happiness than unhappiness would result from a given course of action.

as they have tested it, the theory then fits all the spontaneous ethical judgments in which they all agree. It is natural for them to ask next whether, on this same theory, lying would be also wrong or on the contrary right. Let us suppose that they agree that it is a mode of conduct generally likely to cause more unhappiness than happiness, i.e., that, according to this same theory, lying would be wrong. Then obviously to approve it would be irrational, that is, theoretically incongruous with their disapproval of killing, adultery, stealing, gambling, drunkenness. And "invalidity"—"unwarrantedness," "unjustifiability"—of a given one of one's own spontaneous ethical judgments can mean nothing whatever except theoretical incongruity, in the sense just described, of the given judgment with the rest, or the majority, or the most confident, of one's own spontaneous ethical judgments.

A claim that a judgment thus theoretically incongruous is nevertheless rational and valid could be based only on the proffering of a rival theory, equally capable of explaining and predicting the other judgments but implying that lying is right. If such another theory were offered, then additional predictions implicit in each theory would have to be examined, and a rational choice between them would be a matter of which one predicts truly the greater number or the most confident of the spontaneous approvals and disapprovals in which the persons agree. If both theories predicted them equally, though one still implied that lying is wrong and the other that it is right, then no rational but only an arbitrary choice would be possible between the two theories. This, however, would be a very extraordinary situation, for it is usually very difficult to devise a theory that will imply everything another theory is found to imply, except for one specified thing as to which it has the contrary implication.

8. *One Ethical Theory, or Several?*—The capacity of a given

ethical theory to explain or predict the empirical generalizations with which it concerns itself can be tested by a person
other than the one whose ethical judgments these generalizations represent, provided only that these judgments be made
known to him. Indeed, if they are known to him, he is in
just as good a position to construct a theory of them as is the
person who made the judgments. For as we have seen, the
validity of a theory of these judgments is not a matter of
whether the person (or group) spontaneously making them
believes that, by the given value-predicate, he or they mean
what the theory says this predicate means. It is a matter of
whether the account of its meaning offered by the theory
stands the tests of validity described above (sec. 6) better than
does any rival account. Scientific status for a theory requires
that the theory be susceptible of confirmation or invalidation
by outside critics, and ethical theories are thus susceptible
of this.

But confirmation or disproof of the capacity of an ethical
theory to integrate conceptually the spontaneous ethical
judgments of a given person or group is after all only historical or maieutic criticism. It is internal criticism—criticism
ex concessis; and ordinarily the sort of criticism we make of
ethical theories is not as detached as this. For example, if a
consequence of a given ethical theory were that matricide
is right, we should not ordinarily limit our critical examination of the theory to inquiring whether or not the judgment
that matricide is right turns out in fact to be an additional
one of the spontaneous judgments of the person or group
whose judgments the theory attempts to integrate conceptually. What we should ordinarily say is rather that since
the theory would entail that matricide is right, whereas in
fact it is wrong, the theory is invalid.

But the fact which is the basis of our own assertion, that

in fact (vs. in theory) matricide is wrong, can be only that both we ourselves and the persons to whose decision we submit the justness of our criticism—that is to say, all persons "who count"—spontaneously disapprove of matricide. And criticism on this basis is still criticism *ex concessis*, although the group whose spontaneous judgments we require the theory to fit is now a different and presumably a more inclusive or in some sense more "authoritative" one. Criticism of an ethical theory—or in general, of a philosophical theory—is always unavoidably thus *ex concessis* and therefore *ad hominem*, because the facts with which the theory ultimately concerns itself are facts intrinsically *ab homine*, viz., are appraisals by men. *Ad hominem* is here also *ad rem*.

Accordingly, there would seem to be only two theoretically possible ways to eliminate the plurality of theories (nonrival) which arises from the intrinsic relativity of the facts concerned to a *variety* of individuals or groups. One way would be to take, as the facts which ethical theory is really (vs. has historically been) required to fit, and with which the incongruous facts are to be aligned, the facts consisting of only the spontaneous ethical judgments in which everybody agrees. But it can be confidently asserted that there are no such facts.

The only remaining way to unity of theory—which is a scientific desideratum—is then to postulate that all persons would spontaneously appraise the same thing alike if they were "in the same position,"[5] and then (in the statement of the facts which the unitary theory is to fit), to specify the appraising person or group concerned not denotatively and therefore absolutely, but descriptively and therefore rela-

---

[5] That is, if the information of any given person, his habits, and his relations to the entity appraised were the same as those of a given other person, he would appraise it identically. (This postulate is plausible in matters other than those described as "matters of individual taste").

tionally, by an account of his or its "position" in the sense stated.

That is, the facts which the theory will have to account for will then be stated not in the form, "person or group P makes appraisal A of entity E," but in the form, "any person or group in position P makes appraisal A of entity E." This (by postulation equivalent) way of formulating the same facts eliminates the conceptual irreconcilability which would appear between such facts as that "person P appraises entity E as bad" and "person Q appraises it as good," if the "positions" of P and of Q were assumed to be the same.

A theory capable of integrating conceptually all spontaneous appraisals will thus necessarily be a relativistic theory in a sense analogous to that in which the "relativity theory" in physics is relativistic. It too, that is to say, will eliminate or at least abstract from the individual observer or judge by conceiving the judgment he renders as a function of his "position" as well as of the entity judged. But a unitary theory, precisely because of its necessarily relativistic character, will not imply that it is necessary for some persons to alter their appraisals for the sake of congruousness with the appraisals of other persons. For a given appraisal can be either really congruous or really incongruous with given others only if all of them are appraisals from the same "position"; and persons other than a given individual or group are always *ex hypothesi* at other "positions" at a given time and can only imperfectly imagine his or its "position." A unitary theory will not even imply that it is necessary for a person to alter some of his appraisals for the sake of congruity with the rest of his own appraisals, if they are appraisals made by him from significantly different "positions," or if the appraisals concerned are not functions solely of his "position" but in part also of an additional variable such as "taste" seems to be; for then the various appraisals cannot be said to be really either congruous or incongruous with one another.

9. *Are Ethical Theories Prescriptive?*—Theory is in itself no more prescriptive in ethics than anywhere else, but only predictive. In the natural sciences, the predictions ultimately concern certain perceptually observable facts in nature; in ethics, certain spontaneous ethical judgments, viz., spontaneous approvals and disapprovals. But although there are spontaneous ethical judgments—and the validity of any ethical theory is ultimately tested by reference to some of them—a given spontaneous judgment may come to be repudiated as incongruous with the theory which adequately fits the rest of them, and replaced by its opposite. In such a case a fact which the theory does not fit is being altered to fit the theory. This is genuinely possible here, because the facts with which the theory concerns itself consist of ethical judgments—approvals or disapprovals—and there is such a thing as changing one's judgment. Nothing similar is possible in natural science, where the facts theorized about neither consist of nor are dependent upon human appraisal. To alter a specimen which conflicts with a given biological theory does not save the theory, for the theory in this case predicts not a judgment by man, which he can alter if he wills, but something that nature under specified circumstances produces, no matter what man's wishes may be, and no matter what man may later do to the thing so produced.

But it is essential to note that a theory rationally explaining and predicting the majority of our spontaneous ethical judgments, or the most confident of such judgments, does not prescribe that we modify others of our ethical judgments which clash with the theory. The theory, as such, only informs us of the modifications to be made in these others if we wish them to become rationally congruous with the rest, or the firmest, of our spontaneous ethical judgments. And it is this wish for theoretical integration, if we have it, which prescribes that we make those modifications.

However, the erroneous belief that ethical theory is prescriptive may have another source beside confusion between information as to the changes needed for theoretical integration, and the wish for such integration. The belief may be due instead to the fact that approval or disapproval of something is an implicit or incipient prescription that it be done or not done. Accordingly, ethical theory, being about approvals and disapprovals, is about prescriptions (implicit ones)—not in the sense that it makes any, but only in the sense that it explains and predicts certain ones, and informs us of certain modes of conduct or states of affairs which our wish for theoretical coherence of all our prescriptions (if we have it) prescribes that we prescribe.

10. *Ethical Theories vs. Ethical Principles.*—We have described above a species of conceptual apparatus consisting of a definition of some ethical predicate and of a method for deciding whether any given empirical subject does or does not exemplify the *definiens*. When such a conceptual apparatus is constructed by a person to explain certain of his spontaneous ethical judgments, it constitutes a theory of these judgments; and if it meets the tests of validity for explanatory theories in general, it provides the judging person or group with the information they need to make their judgments, in cases where they are in doubt, theoretically coherent with the spontaneous ones the theory explains and predicts.

But the manner in which such a conceptual apparatus comes to be adopted may be very different from this. Instead of being constructed by a person or group for himself or

itself, it may be presented ready-made to their minds by somebody else, and be adopted not at all because of any explanatory power it may have, but simply because the psychological
manner of its presentation—be this suggestion, sugar-
coating, pressure, or anything else—is psychologically
adequate for getting it adopted by them. In such a case that
conceptual apparatus can no longer be described as for them a
theory explanatory of given spontaneous judgments. It is
rather a principle of ethical judgment. It is a general rule for
determining what sorts of things to approve and disapprove—
a general rule for arriving at specific ethical norms.

Adoption of it insures unity of principle in ethical judgments derived from it, but question arises as to what other sort
of merit, if any, it may have. Evidently it does not have that
of explaining or predicting the spontaneous judgments of
the person who has adopted it, since it was not desired to do
this and rather censors or supersedes them. Such a rule of
judgment can only have the merit of being a means to an end
desired by whoever urged or forced its adoption. And it is
difficult to see what sort of end this could be other than to
bring about or to prevent—through the ethical judgments
dictated by adoption of the rule—situations respectively
approved or disapproved spontaneously by the person who
urges adoption of the rule.

When a child adopts a rule from his parents, the situations
which the parents aim to bring about or prevent are ones
that they spontaneously approve or disapprove, and believe
the child also will later respectively approve and disapprove
spontaneously. Where adoption of a rule is psychologically
enforced by a tyrant upon his subjects, the situations intended
are ones that he himself spontaneously approves, or disapproves notwithstanding that he knows that his subjects
appraise them differently. But in any case, adoption of a rule

or enforcement of it on someone is rationally defensible only by reference to expected fruits consisting of situations spontaneously approved or disapproved by some specified person or persons. If no spontaneous approvals and disapprovals existed, no set of maxims for conduct, be they ever so coherent in principle, would have anything whatever to recommend it over any different but equally coherent set. Even when a philosophical theory or principle is free from formal defects, an appeal—initial or terminal—to philosophical experience is thus indispensable for validating or invalidating it. On the other hand, philosophical experience without philosophical theory would remain as precarious, as poor in content, and as limited in applicability as would physics if deprived of physical theory and confined to empirical generalizations.

It is worth noting that ethical theory can serve only to make future conduct theoretically coherent with past or present ethical experience. It might be that the remote consequences of something we spontaneously disapprove are of a sort we would approve strongly enough to make us approve instead of disapprove what brought it about if we knew that it has these remote consequences. If we do not know this, theorizing will never inform us of it. The only thing that would inform us of it would be observation that the remote consequences are of that sort. If such information were sought experimentally, the experiments would, let it be noted, consist in deliberately doing something which both spontaneous judgment and theory based on this pronounce wrong, in order to find out whether consequences of it more remote than theory has yet taken into account may not be of a sort that would ultimately lead us to pronounce the act or situation right instead of wrong. Since this does sometimes turn out to be the case, there is in the field of ethics justification for a certain amount of experimentation flying in the face of past experience and of theory based on it—for a certain amount of adventure or exploratory conduct *prima facie* unethical instead of prudent or ethical.

11. *Experience and Theory in Branches of Philosophy Other than Ethics.*—What has been said concerning the relation in ethics between theory and given general facts (whether directly obtained from primitive or from derivative facts) applies equally, *mutatis mutandis*, to branches of philosophy other than ethics. This may be shown by considering briefly one or two examples relating to the theory of knowledge. It is well to bear in mind, however, something already emphasized, viz., that theories, in philosophy as elsewhere, and in the theory of knowledge as in ethics, are more often directly about derivative facts of the given field than directly about its primitives, and that therefore, although appraisals are the primitive facts of philosophy, most of the terms as to the meaning of which philosophy is called upon to frame explanatory hypotheses are not themselves terms of appraisal but rather stand for things implicit in appraisals and brought out by prior study of the latter. This prior study, moreover, may to some extent or in some cases have been automatic rather than deliberate, and made by generations past rather than by ourselves, its results then being matters of "common-sense knowledge" rather than of esoteric and technical knowledge. We shall here, however, as in the case of ethics, take terms of appraisal as examples, because to do so will stress the fact that doubt of given appraisals is what originally generates philosophical theorizing.

As an example of a spontaneous judgment of appraisal in the field of the theory of knowledge, we may take this: "The inference that, since all men are mortal and all vertebrates are mortal, therefore all men are vertebrates, is fallacious." This appraisal can be regarded as spontaneous in the sense already specified. That is, it is an appraisal that would be made by many persons who, although logically sensitive, are wholly ignorant of syllogistic theory. If this appraisal were disputed, the question would immediately arise as to what exactly is being predicated of that inference when it is called "fallacious." Any answer constituting an explanation of the appraisal (whether tenable or untenable), will be one from which it would be logically possible to deduce the fallaciousness not only of the given inference, but also of some other spontaneous inferences resembling it more or less closely. That is, it will be an explanation not exclusively of the particular fact that the given inference is fallacious, but essentially of an empirically ascertainable general fact, that is, an empirical law—for instance, of the law that all inferences of the form "all S is M, all P is M, therefore all S is P" are fallacious. The theory consisting of the definition, "A fallacious inference is an inference in which the middle term is undistributed," and of the method of identification, "The middle term is the term which occurs in both premises, and a term is undistributed if it is predicate of an affirmative proposition or subject of a particular proposition," would explain that empirical law and demonstrate, as a case under it, the fallaciousness of the given inference.

But if the appraisal of that inference as fallacious were defended in this way, the objection would very likely be made that although the theory of fallaciousness stated does rationally justify that appraisal and some others, there are many other inferences appraised also as fallacious, the fallaciousness of which is not accounted for by that theory. To integrate these other appraisals with the given one, a more comprehensive theory would have to be produced. It might be the traditional syllogistic theory; or, since not all inferences are syllogistic, some still more comprehensive one might be needed to account for all the spontaneous appraisals of fallaciousness taken as data. A theory adequate to do this would doubtless also reveal the fallaciousness of some inferences in cases where one found one's self unable to make a confident spontaneous appraisal.

Other terms of epistemic appraisal, such as "sound" and "erroneous," "correct" and "incorrect," etc., could be taken as examples, and the relation of philosophical theory to primitive philosophical experience illustrated in terms of them in a similar manner. But perhaps the most comprehensive terms of epistemic appraisal we could consider would be "knowledge" and "ignorance." It is true that, like other terms illustrated in the discussion of the relation of appraisal to description in chapter x, they can be and sometimes are applied without import of appraisal; but in the large majority of cases, when we declare an opinion to have the status of knowledge, a part at least of what we mean by this is that it is better than—superior to—certain others (which we might appraise more specifically as erroneous, or as possibly sound but unproved, etc.) and better also than absence of opinion, or of opinion having the status of knowledge, on the same subject. Doubt or dispute as to whether or not a given opinion does have the status of knowledge would—in cases where additional examination of the data of the opinion does not settle the matter—automatically bring up the question as to what exactly we are predicating of an opinion when we appraise it as being knowledge; and the whole of the theory of knowledge develops, in the general manner already repeatedly illustrated, out of the attempt to answer this question.

That most of its familiar problems are derivative from this question about its primitives is obvious if we consider any plausible answer to it. For example, if the answer is proposed that knowledge is the status an opinion has if and only if it is based upon evidence sufficient to prove its soundness, then the need to specify a method by which to determine whether or not any given opinion is so based forces us to consider what exactly an opinion is, how opinions are related to propositions, and how the soundness or erroneousness of opinions relates to the truth or falsity of propositions; what propositions themselves are, and what their truth or falsity consists in; what is meant by saying that an opinion is "based upon" evidence; what sort of thing is capable of serving as "evidence"; what is the test of the "sufficiency" of given evidence to prove the soundness of a given opinion; how proof and probability are related, etc. All these questions, and many others that are admittedly philosophical but seem to have no connection with appraisals, are thus implicit in the initial question as to what is predicated of an opinion when it is appraised as being knowledge. Any attempt to answer the initial question exhaustively brings out all these, and thereby demonstrates that they are derivative from a question about appraisal.

CHAPTER THIRTEEN

Philosophy, Wisdom, and the
Application of Wisdom

ETYMOLOGICALLY, "philosophy" means the love of wisdom, but the term has always been used to designate an activity rather than an emotion—the activity, then, of searching for wisdom. The love of wisdom is thus not philosophy itself; rather, the love of wisdom, or perhaps more accurately the felt need for wisdom, is what originally drives man to philosophize. What exactly, however, is this "wisdom" that philosophy seeks? Is it a species of knowledge? If so, what distinguishes it from knowledge in general? I submit that wisdom is knowledge of norms and that philosophy therefore, conceived in terms of the sort of need that originates it, is the search for knowledge of norms.

1. *Wisdom as Knowledge of Norms.*—Norms are truths concerning the value—positive or negative—of given kinds of things. They are expressed by statements of the form (or of any form equivalent to) "anything of kind K has value V," where "having value V" stands, as the case may be, for being good, or wrong, or valid, or erroneous, or sublime, or inexpedient, or holy, or wise, or incorrect, etc. An example of a manner of stating norms equivalent to that just given, and frequently used, would be: "Things of kind K ought (or

ought not) to be" or, as the case may be, "ought (or ought not) to be done," or "asserted," or "believed," or "felt," etc.

In the preceding chapter, "stealing is wrong," "killing is wrong," and "adultery is wrong," were given as examples of statements of norms of social conduct. These statements would also commonly be described as statements purporting to embody bits of wisdom. This supports the contention that wisdom is knowledge of norms, which is further supported by the fact that the maxims, proverbs, aphorisms, or rules which are generally regarded as the sorts of statements by means of which wisdom (whether genuine or spurious) is expressed, all essentially purport to formulate guides to the obtaining of positive value or to the avoiding of negative value. Among other examples may be mentioned the maxims attributed to one or another of the seven wise men of Greece, such as "Know thyself" or "Do nothing in excess"; or bits of homespun wisdom current today, such as "A penny saved is a penny earned" or "One stitch in time saves nine"; or proverbs given by William Blake as embodying the wisdom of hell, such as "If the fool would persist in his folly, he would become wise," etc.

But beside norms for conduct in everyday life—which like those above often are expressed in aphoristic manner—there are others of a more technical nature. Examples would be the rules of scientific method, of artistic creation in this or that medium, of valid and invalid reasoning; the conditions upon which beauty or ugliness in given sorts of objects depends for given persons; the statements of the various religions as to what wins or loses for man heaven, nirvana, or salvation; also legal statutes and the rules of successful (or unsuccessful) procedure in medicine, advertising, building, manufacturing, or other practical arts. The statements of any of these may be described indifferently as statements of claimed norms; or as statements of characters of things or of manners of procedure upon which the presence or the eventuation of value or of disvalue is claimed to depend; or, lastly, as statements of pieces of claimed wisdom. The three descriptions are synonymous, and this confirms that, as contended, wisdom is knowledge of norms.

From the examples given, it is evident that there are positive and negative norms—"ought's" and "ought not's"; and also that the statement of a norm may be a statement of something sufficient for the attainment of the given sort of value, or of something necessary to it, or of something both sufficient for and necessary to it. In the great majority of cases, however, it is the statement of a character sufficient for negative value, or of a character necessary to positive value. In target shooting, for instance, pulling the trigger jerkily is sufficient but not necessary to make the manner of shooting bad; and pulling it smoothly is necessary but not sufficient to make it good.

2. *Norms Distinguished from Aims and Desiderata.*—Before inquiring further into the relation of philosophy to wisdom, it is important to guard against the tempting confusion between a norm and a desideratum or an aim. In target shooting, for instance, the aim is to hit the bull's-eye, but the norms are truths as to the manner of holding the gun, pulling the trigger, etc.—that is, as to manners of target shooting, which tend to result in, or to prevent, hitting the bull's-eye. Thus, "to pull the trigger sharply is wrong," "to hold the gun steady is right," would be statements of some norms of target shooting. In the activity called chess playing, the aim is to checkmate the opponent's king, but the norms consist of general truths concerning ways of playing one's pieces

that tend to bring about, or to defeat, this aim. The aim of
the sort of activity called research is to attain knowledge,
but the norms of it are truths as to ways of performing it
which generally result in, or thwart, the attainment of
knowledge, as, "the sample on which an induction is based
ought to be large and taken at random"; "a syllogistic
inference in which the middle term is undistributed is fallacious," etc. Or again, to consider cases not of telic activities
directly, but of things which are implements of or desiderata
in telic activities, the function of a razor blade—the desiderated operation which it implements—is to shave, but norms
for razor blades would be truths as to attributes of blades on
which adequate performance of this function depends, as,
"unless a razor blade is sharp, it is not good"; or, otherwise
expressed, "a razor blade ought to be sharp."

3. *Knowledge of Norms Used to Define Specific Aims for Censorial
Activity.*—Although strictly speaking a norm is not and
cannot be an aim, knowledge of norms defines specific aims
for purposive activity of a certain sort, namely, for emendatory or, more inclusively, censorial activity. Knowledge of
the norms for a given sort of activity or object sometimes
makes evident that the activity or the object is actually
defective in form, i.e., does not conform to its norms. One
can then attempt to alter its form so as to "normalize" it.[1]
Activity which thus aims to improve the form either of some
other activity or of some object is emendatory activity, and
knowledge of the norms of that other activity or object is

[1] To normalize is to render (or maintain) normal; and "normal" is used here
throughout in the sense of "as ought to be," i.e., "conforming to the norm or ideal"
for the given kind of entity or of purposive activity. That is, normal is not used
here in the looser sense of "as generally is," or "as habitually." The habitual, or the
most frequent, or the average, may or may not happen to be also the normal in
the stricter sense of conforming to the norm, i.e., of "having the form which is
best" for the kind of entity or of purposive activity concerned.

knowledge of the specific form which emendatory activity aims to impose on the other activity or object.

Knowledge of the norms for this other activity or object, however, may reveal that actually its form is not defective but on the contrary normal. In such a case, there is no call to emend it, but only to preserve it. But the activity which consists in either bringing about or preserving conformity of something to the norms for that thing is censorial activity. We may therefore say that the utility—the value as means, the practical value—of knowledge of norms consists in its capacity to dictate what censorial activity is specifically to aim at in given kinds of cases.

4. *Censorial Activity Not Philosophy but Philosophical Engineering.*—To criticize is to judge as to the conformity or non-conformity of something to its norms. To censor is to bring about or to maintain such conformity. Censoring may thus be described as philosophical engineering, that is, as the sort of activity which constitutes practical application of philosophical knowledge. At least, it is philosophical engineering when the censoring is carried on in the light of (more or less probable and approximate) knowledge of norms, as distinguished from merely imitative acceptance of alleged norms, and from faith in the sense of belief in certain norms which exceeds in degree what the available evidence for them rationally justifies.

The task of the philosophical engineer is then to apply knowledge of norms to the control of the form of the activities or objects for which they are the norms. These activities or objects may be his own, or those of another person such as a child or a student whom he is called upon to supervise, or those of an institution or of a portion of society, etc. And they may be of any sort—scientific, artistic, recreational, economic, political, educational, or other.

But the fact that philosophical knowledge does have practicability of a specific sort, and that the task of applying it is of great importance, leaves untouched the difference between the task of the philosophical investigator and that of the philosophical engineer, and therefore does not justify the identification of philosophy with philosophical engineering to which some eminent pragmatists are prone, nor the disparagement of the theoretical part of philosophy to which this mistake leads them.

5. *Censorables Possibly Qualities, Telic Activities, or Instruments.*—There is no such thing as a norm for an entity considered out of relation to any appraising being, since a norm is a proposition concerning the sort of appraisal some person or persons make of a given sort of entity. But endlessly various as are the entities we appraise, they automatically fall, in respect to appraisal, into one or another of three categories. We may call these the three kinds of censorables. Appraisal may be, namely, of some quality, or of the form of some telic activity, or of some instrument (positive or negative) to a given end. It might be thought that the use to which a given instrument is put, and the end of a given telic activity, would be two additional categories of censorables; but any appraisal we make of a use or of an end either is of this as itself an instrument to some ulterior end, or is an appraisal of the intrinsic nature of this use or end. If for example we condemn a use made by a man of his money, for instance a use consisting of bribery of some official, what we condemn is either bribery itself, considered qualitatively (i.e., we dislike it) or bribery considered as instrument—in this case negative instrument, i.e., obstacle—to some end we value positively. Or if we condemn the end of some telic activity, e.g., the end consisting of being very rich, we are either considering the

possession of great riches itself, qualitatively, and find that we simply dislike the sort of thing it is; or we are considering it as instrument to some end—perhaps social or spiritual—that we value positively, and find that it is a negative instrument, i.e., an obstacle, to it.

We need now to clarify further the difference assumed above between a telic activity and a means or instrument, and to consider with some care the general nature of telism and its kinds. This will enable us to discern what exactly is the relation between wisdom, i.e., knowledge of norms, which philosophy seeks, and knowledge of the laws of nature or other nonaxiological laws.

6. *The Nature of Telism.*—Telism is a special case of causation; but it emphatically does not consist, as sometimes alleged, in causation of an earlier event by a later. If one observes carefully some undoubted cases of telism, one finds them to be cases where not the later occurrence of an event E, but the earlier occurrence of desire for the later occurrence of E, causes performance of an act A, which itself then causes E (either directly or through an instrument). That is, performance of act A at time 2 by person P is not caused by occurrence of E at time 3; it is caused by P's desire at time 1 that E shall occur at time 3. What is true, however, is that, for a spectator, occurrence of E at time 3 explains performance of A by P at time 2. But it explains that performance not by exhibiting itself as cause of it, but by exhibiting itself as something occurring indeed at time 3, desire for which by P at time 1 would have been sufficient to cause, and probably did cause, performance of A by P at time 2.

7. *Telism vs. Automatic Mechanical Regulation.*[2]—The claim

---

[2] I shall use "mechanical" to describe cases where the cause of an event (under the circumstances prevailing at the time) is not a desire for the event.

is sometimes made that in biology one finds cases where the supposition of antecedent desire as cause is not plausible, which are nevertheless cases of telism; for example, maintenance of the proportion of blood salts to blood volume, or maintenance of the temperature of the blood. What leads to description of them as cases of telism is doubtless that in them one finds, in spite of variations in earlier circumstances, the same constancy in a later event that antecedent desire for that event would explain; and that, since no antecedent desire is discoverable in these cases, the only possible remaining explanation seems to be causation of the earlier events by the later. But there is a third possible explanation which does not require this absurdity, namely, explanation of these cases as cases of automatic mechanical regulation.

In automatic mechanical regulation, disturbance of an equilibrium happens to be the very thing that mechanically causes restoration of the equilibrium, so that the latter remains constant within more or less close limits.[3] Cases of maintenance of equilibrium which everybody would grant as being of this kind would be that of a tank equipped with a ball float so connected with an intake valve that the valve admits water when the level falls, thus maintaining the level within certain limits; or the case of an oil-burning heating system equipped with a thermostat, which maintains the temperature within certain limits.

It may be said, of course, that these mechanisms are not, like the bodies of animals, also self-repairing or self-feeding. But this is a matter of degree. Machines exist in which the wear that occurs at least at certain points is automatically taken up, perhaps by a spring that keeps a movable bearing

---

[3] This sort of explanation would be excluded only if the equilibrium remained absolutely and not only approximately constant; for, if minute variations from the equilibrium did not occur, they could not be causes of its restoration or its constancy.

in contact with a shaft until nothing is left of the bearing. This automatic compensation for wear, of course, has its limits, but so has that of animal bodies. In the latter, the variety of contingencies for which mechanisms for automatic maintenance exist is enormously greater, but even then we know only too well that they have limits, and that when these are exceeded, death or permanent crippling results. As regards self-feeding, an oil burner has a mechanism by which it automatically "feeds" itself oil when it needs some, under certain circumstances, viz., when there is oil in the tank. The body, similarly, feeds itself when it needs food, provided there is food within the reach of the food-getting equipment it possesses. If that equipment is not adequate or if there is no food, the body, like the heating system, ceases to function.

It may be said that a water tank with a ball float, a heating system, etc., are after all constructed by activity which is purposive. But although this is true, the question as to how they came to exist, and the question whether they effect maintenance of an equilibrium in a purely mechanical manner, are distinct questions. The latter must of course be answered in the affirmative. As regards the former, it is worth noting that examples can be found where an equilibrium is automatically maintained by purely mechanical means, and where purpose has nevertheless had no part. The flow of the water of a river towards the sea, for example, maintains itself automatically. If a rock slide obstructs the flow, it automatically raises the water level, and this either builds up an increase of water pressure sufficient to clear the channel, or it causes the water to find a new outlet.

We cannot say that in the presence of an obstruction the water rises in order to, i.e., because it purposes to, continue towards the sea, but only that unless it does rise, it does not so continue. Similarly, we cannot say that in the water tank with float-connected valve, the valve opens proportionately to the fall of the level in order that, i.e., because it desires that, the loss be compensated by the intake, but only that unless it opens proportionately, the loss is not compensated. And in the body, likewise, we cannot say that, e.g., it perspires in the presence of a rise in the temperature of the air in order to, i.e., because it desires to, maintain constant the temperature of the blood, but only that unless the body perspires the temperature of the blood goes up. In all these cases alike, what we have are physical regulatory mechanisms which automatically maintain a phenomenon in the face of disturbing causes, so long as the disturbing causes are of certain kinds and do not exceed certain quantitative limits. The regulation is, so far as we can see, susceptible of being eventually explained in these biological cases in the same kind of terms as in the nonbiological, i.e., in physicochemical terms and without the supposition of purpose.

Haldane, it is true, shows that organisms differ from machines in certain respects.[4] In organisms, for instance, there is reciprocal regulation of the parts, even including their structure, by one another, so that they cannot be separated from one another without being thereby altered. Again, there is reciprocal regulation of the organism and its environment (both internal and external) by each other, so that the organism cannot be separated from its environment without being thereby altered. Again, in organisms the maintenance of certain functions goes far beyond any point reached in machines, even being effected in ways that are new on occasions when the ordinary ways of maintenance are impeded.

To say that they are new, however, does not imply that they are not purely physical. It may quite well mean only that they represent the coming into play of physical mechan-

[4] *Organism and Environment* (1917).

isms present in the organisms all along, but which, like the safety valve of a boiler, come into play only on kinds of occasions that are rare, or possibly unique, in the history of a given organism. Haldane, moreover, does not show that regulation of the reciprocal kind, which we find in connection with organisms, cannot be explained in physicochemical terms; he shows only that if the explanation is physicochemical, it is exceedingly complex and very far from completely known to us as yet. He does not show, in short, that even the kinds of difference he points out between organisms and machines are not ultimately analyzable into differences of degree.

8. *Categories of Telic Activity.*—Telic activities may be classified on the basis of the general nature of what is purposed; and labels for the resulting species could if needed be coined to fit. What is purposed may be, for instance, the acquisition of some power, or of knowledge of certain facts, or the experience of some feeling, emotion, or other affective state—in each case either by one's self (egocentric) or by someone else (altrocentric). Further, the end desired may be more or less determinate. A boy shaking a tree may be moved by desire for one particular apple, or for an apple, or for some fruit—or, still more indeterminately, for something exciting to happen.

Telic activities, however, may be classified also on the basis of the relation of the end desired to the activity itself. In play activities, which have been described as autotelic, the ostensible end is pursued essentially because the pursuing activity is itself enjoyed, so that enjoyment of it is the real end. Compare for instance fishing for fun with fishing for food. The latter would be heterotelic, in that the activity, even if it happens to be enjoyed, is not performed for the sake of the enjoyment as end. It would be, further, "practical," in the sense that what is desired, viz., food, is an instrument to an ulterior end (viz., cessation or prevention of hunger), and not itself a terminal desideratum. It is in this respect that the activities classed as work, or labor, i.e., as practical, differ from those classed as artistic, or more inclusively, self-expressive. For in the latter the object one attempts to create is a terminal, not an intermediary, desideratum. It is created because one desires it to exist, not because of what one might desire to use it for after it has been created.

Further, telic activity—and only activity which is telic—is skilled or (relatively) unskilled. It is skilled—wise of its kind—in so far as the specific form of it is controlled by knowledge of the norms for its kind, that is, by knowledge of the specific form of it that insures attainment of its end. But even striving for a given end by "trial and error" is not usually completely unskilled striving. If for example one purposes to open a locked door, one may not know which key in the bunch is the "normal" key, but one would usually know that to say "Open sesame," or to twiddle one's thumbs in front of the door, are abnormal—wrong—ways of attempting to open it, and that although "to insert some key in the lock and turn" is a not sufficiently determinate description of the form of activity appropriate to the end, it nevertheless describes a form of activity which is normal—right—so far as it goes. Knowledge of this restricts the variety of forms of activity one tries at random. Telic activity, thus, is hardly ever absolutely but rather only relatively unskilled.

9. *Relation of Knowledge of the Laws of Nature to Wisdom.*— A given manner of striving for a given end cannot be described as normal or abnormal without reference to the circumstances under which it is performed. Simply turning the knob of a

door is the normal way of attempting to open the door when it is not locked, but not when it is. The normal form of a telic activity (aiming at end E) must therefore be described as the form of it which, *under circumstances of kind* K, regularly results in E. Wisdom, therefore, necessarily takes circumstances into account: what is wisdom here is foolishness there, and wise is he only who knows where is where!

Attention to this fact enables us now to discern exactly how knowledge of the laws of nature, or in general of non-axiological laws, is related to knowledge of norms, that is, to wisdom. Our analysis of telic activity distinguished therein (1) desire at time 1 that an event of kind E occur at time 3; (2) causation by this desire of a certain form of activity A at time 2; and (3) causation by this activity of event E at time 3. But A may cause E either directly or indirectly. If event E is, for instance, cessation of an itchy feeling at the tip of one's nose, and activity A is scratching the tip of one's nose, then A causes E directly, that is, without the use of an instrument. But if E is the opening of the door of a house other than one's own, and activity A is pressing upon the bell button, A causes E indirectly, viz., by causing the button to move, which causes the bell to ring, which causes some one to come and open the door. That is, A then causes E only by means of an instrument. An instrument is an object I which, when acted upon in a manner A by man, behaves in a certain manner M, this behavior being either the desiderated event E itself, or an event which in turn causes another object J to behave in a manner N, this behavior of J then being either the desired event E itself or, etc. This means that when A does not cause E directly, its causing E at all is dependent upon the properties of certain objects in the environment (which constitute the *circumstances* under which A is performed).

We can therefore say that knowledge of the properties of

things in nature is knowledge of the sorts of external circumstances under which a given form of an activity A (telic to a given sort of end E) is normal, i.e., successful. This knowledge is applicable to the task of implementing the activities we are already capable of performing—the skills or powers we already possess. It is not applicable to the task of self-improvement—of acquisition of new powers or of perfecting those we already have in some degree. Throwing a life preserver to a sinking person implements the power to grasp, which he already possesses, in such manner as to make it indirectly adequate—normal—to his end of staying afloat; but it does not confer upon him a new power, such as swimming skill, or normalize the thrashing motions by which he strives to stay afloat.

The sort of knowledge philosophy seeks, on the other hand, is knowledge of the specific form which, under circumstances of a given kind, i.e., with given instruments, or without any instruments, is the normal form of an activity A telic to a sort of end E. Knowledge of this sort is applicable to the task of self-perfection—to the normalizing of activities we are already capable of but the specific form of which is inadequate to our ends under the existing circumstances, or to the development of new powers normal to our ends under the circumstances we have to face.

The problem constituted by incapacity to obtain a desired end is susceptible of being solved in three ways. They are the practical way, "implement the powers you have"; the philosophical way, "develop the powers you need"; and the religious way, which is that of resignation, "give up the ends you desire—learn to say, 'Not my will, but Thine.'"

10. *Wisdom and Technical Philosophy.*—To illuminate further the relation between wisdom, which is knowledge of norms,

and philosophy, conceived as the search for this knowledge, let us consider next how this search may proceed. Here we recall what was said earlier concerning the relation of theory to laws in general, and therefore also to axiological laws, that is, to laws that are norms. They may be discovered in two ways.

One way is directly by inductive generalization from particular experiences, which in philosophy consist of spontaneous appraisals of particular things. Philosophical generalizations so obtained are empirical norms and knowledge of them is empirical wisdom. The thought-processes by which it is obtained from the spontaneous particular appraisals that are the philosophical raw material are the same as those through which empirical generalizations about anything else are obtained: comparisons of the given things with one another, discrimination of their kinds through discernment of likenesses and differences, the tracing of kinds of effects to kinds of causes, generalization from the observed cases of given kinds to all cases of these kinds.

These thought-processes, when they have spontaneous particular appraisals as their raw material, constitute empirical philosophizing. Empirical philosophizing is ordinarily motivated directly by a felt need for wisdom. It is carried on, although only sporadically and without scientific precautions, by many persons who know nothing of technical philosophy, indeed, at least in small degree and at a few times, by almost every person. Such wisdom as it yields is embodied in the common maxims, proverbs, and counsels of which examples have already been cited and, for conduct in situations of more specialized sorts, in various "rules of thumb."

But the wisdom which empirical philosophizing brings is as precarious as are the products of purely empirical generalization in any other field. This wisdom, that is to say, will concern only situations more or less stereotyped and of relatively simple kinds. It will tend to be wisdom for the relatively short run rather than the long. It will be valid for the average man but perhaps not for the man who is exceptional in certain respects. Its maxims, moreover, will seldom be very precise. Certain cases will clearly fall within the scope of any given one of them, and certain other cases clearly outside it; but many others will be left neither definitely in nor definitely out. Empirical wisdom tells us, for example, that stealing is wrong, but it does not tell exactly where "stealing" begins and "finding" ends. Some instances are clearly cases of the one and some clearly of the other; but others are doubtful. For example, A sees B, who is walking a quarter of a mile or so ahead, drop his purse. It is a hot day, and the purse is worthless and contains only one penny; A has a weak heart, and he does not attempt to catch B but keeps the penny. Is this stealing and therefore wrong, or is it finding and blameless? The maxim that stealing is wrong does not answer this question.

The loose and unsystematic way in which the scope of the maxims of empirical wisdom is defined results not only in examples like this, where a given case seems not to fit exactly into either one of two rival categories, but also in examples where a given case seems definitely to fit into two of them. The often-mentioned possible alternative between saving a life through lying, and telling the truth at the cost of loss of that life, would be an example. Empirical wisdom seldom if ever has maxims to cover cases of clash between its own common maxims, or cases of other unusual or complicated kinds. But wisdom—knowledge of the values of kinds of things—is poor indeed unless it includes knowledge also of their relative values; and little of this knowledge is to be obtained by purely empirical generalization from spontaneous appraisals.

Accordingly, for wisdom of the firmer and more discriminating and resourceful sort, which is applicable not only to stereotyped situations but also to novel or otherwise puzzling ones, we have to turn to the other way of discovering norms, namely, to deduction from theory. As we have seen, theory which has proved adequate to explain and predict empirical norms is also adequate to define more sharply the rational scope of their validity, to settle rationally conflicts between them, and to discover rationally defensible norms for novel situations.

The conceptual apparatus of which a philosophical theory consists, and the processes by which it is constructed, have already been described. They include tentative definition of the particular philosophical predicate with which the theory is concerned, tentative specification of a method for identifying cases of what has thus been defined, testing the validity of those constructs empirically by reference to particular philosophical facts already known (primitive or derivative, as the case may be), and making systematically explicit whatever is implicit in the theory so constructed, once its validity has been sufficiently tested. Some of the things implicit in it are axiological laws, i.e., norms, which are then describable as rational norms or theoretically grounded norms, in contrast to the purely and directly empirical ones mentioned above. These processes together constitute philosophical theorizing or, if we prefer, theoretical philosophizing as distinguished from the purely empirical philosophizing already described.

This theoretical part of the search for knowledge of norms is—like search for knowledge of anything else through theory construction—much more abstract and technical and indirect than the immediately empirical part. To it belongs the bulk of what is found in most philosophical treatises. Written or otherwise explicit philosophizing—whether in a given instance valid or fallacious—consists in searching for wisdom in that way, viz., through theory construction. The philosophizing which consists in induction directly from spontaneous particular appraisals, and the results of which are formulated in maxims of empirical wisdom, is usually not itself formulated at all; or when it is, it is formulated not in treatises but in fables, myths, or other stories with a moral.

Because the theoretical part of the search for knowledge of norms is, as stated above, far more technical, indirect, and abstract than the immediately empirical part, it is ordinarily motivated chiefly by the interest that the processes of theory construction and theory testing themselves directly have for the persons who perform them, and only remotely, or in some of these persons perhaps not at all, by any felt need for wisdom wherewith to normalize practice. This, moreover, is in no way improper, for the task they perform is an indispensable one, and the right motivation for it is any motivation that does get it performed.

The fruitfulness of theories, furthermore—whether in philosophy or in natural or formal science—does not depend on the motive that leads to their construction, but on their technical perfection and on the rigor with which their validity is empirically tested. Pragmatists have urged that the most fruitful way of acquiring knowledge is through doing, and that for philosophy this means seeking specifically for the wisdom that will enable us to solve the social or moral problems of our epoch. But if this injunction warns philosophers away from anything, it is from seeking wisdom through theory construction rather than through direct observation and experiment; and—since technically defective theory construction is not advocated by anybody—this is to condemn theory construction in general as a method of seeking knowledge.

But that theorizing is in fact a far more powerful method than is direct experimentation unguided by theory is overwhelmingly proved by the history of the natural sciences. When this is pointed out, however, pragmatists are wont to retort that they do not condemn theory construction, but contend that attainment of any knowledge—even of the most abstract and technical theoretical knowledge—consists in solution of some problem; and that this—the solving of some problem or, as they may put it, the successful dealing with some "problem situation"—is what "learning by doing" essentially consists in. But then, if this is the only way in which knowledge can be obtained, it is automatically the way that always has been used, whether consciously or unconsciously, by anybody who has gained any knowledge, whether natural, philosophical, or other, and whether he was "empiricist" or "rationalist," naïve observer, experimenter, or theorist. To advocate its use is thus as idle as it would be to advocate the use of breathing by men who seek to remain alive. We may well ask, then, what exactly the pragmatist's counsel reduces to, if not to a counsel of perfection—the counsel, namely, to succeed in one's attempt to solve the problems, whether theoretical or directly empirical, to which one addresses one's self!

CHAPTER FOURTEEN

The Method of Knowledge in Philosophy

IN THIS chapter, I propose to summarize and to supplement at a number of points the conclusions that have gradually been reached in the preceding discussion concerning philosophy and its method.

Our initial postulate, it will be recalled, was that philosophy resembles the natural and other sciences in being essentially a knowledge-seeking enterprise. This entails that its method must be "scientific," that is, knowledge-yielding; and scientific method in general—as distinguished from the particular procedures dictated by application of it to particular sorts of subject matter—may be characterized broadly as involving scrutiny of data (so far as possible under experimental conditions), empirical generalization, explanatory theorizing, empirical testing of the theories constructed, and organization of the validated theories belonging to the given field of inquiry into a logically complete whole.[1] As a product of the construction of valid theory, additional laws of the

[1] Experimental scrutiny is essentially observation of the differential outcome of an operation, i.e., of the outcome of that operation alone. The operation may be performed by ourselves (as in the laboratory use of the "method of difference," or, in mathematics, of the operation which, performed upon a number, reveals whether or not it is divisible by 7); or the operation may be performed by nature (as for instance in an eclipse).

given field, too exact or too recondite to have been discovered by direct generalization of observations, are usually obtained. That these are the essential features of knowledge-yielding method would probably be granted so far as the natural sciences are concerned; and something has been said to show that they may be traced also in the procedures of the formal sciences, and what forms they assume in those sciences.

To vindicate the contention that these features also characterize knowledge-yielding method in philosophy, what was needed was similarly to make clear what specific forms they assume where the subject matter about which knowledge is sought is philosophical.

1. *The Facts of Observation in Philosophy.*—For this it was first of all necessary to determine what exactly is the subject matter distinctive of philosophy. To do this we were forced to distinguish between the primitive and the derivative facts of any knowledge-seeking enterprise, and we found that the subject matter distinctive of any given such enterprise is ultimately to be defined in terms of the sort of facts the enterprise takes as primitive. The facts primitive for philosophy, it was asserted, consist of spontaneous particular appraisals, in so far as made available for public study through veracious formulation of them. That they consist of appraisals was evidenced on the one hand by pointing out that philosophy is generally thought of as being the search for wisdom, and that the maxims or aphorisms in which wisdom is typically formulated state, either directly or by implication, appraisals of various kinds of things; and on the other hand, by pointing out that theorizing of the kind generally called philosophical is what automatically occurs when one attempts to settle rationally a doubt or dispute of a spontaneous appraisal.

Formulated spontaneous appraisals of particular entities

(which entities may be acts, objects, situations, thought-processes, feelings, or anything else) are thus the philosophical analogues of the publicly perceived particular facts that are primitive for natural science, and are accordingly what primitive philosophical experience, or primitive facts of observation in philosophy, consist in. But in philosophy as in natural science, there are facts of observation which, although still particular, are derivative instead of primitive. This is the case whenever a character observed in a given particular entity is of a kind implicit in a certain kind of primitive character present in this entity—that is, derivative in the sense that the former kind of character was originally discerned through interpretive reflection upon primitives of the latter kind.

This reflection, however, may have been performed not by us but by someone else, and its results then directly or indirectly imparted to us by him. This means that a character familiar to us may be derivative and yet not have been derived by us. As Whewell emphasizes, something which yesterday would have been called "interpretation of a perceived fact" is today called "perception of a fact" if in the meantime the interpretation has been tested and validated and has become habitual. The physicist, for instance, will say not that he perceived a streak in the vapor of a cloud-chamber, but that he perceived the emission of an electron. Or, to take a less esoteric example, we say that we perceive the sun being eclipsed by the moon, instead of saying that we perceive the shape of the sun gradually changing from a circle to a crescent that diminishes to nothing.

Similarly in philosophy, we must distinguish between primitive philosophical characters, which are the various value-characters, and derivative philosophical characters, which are the ones implicit in the value-characters. For example, "being erroneous" is a primitive philosophical character. But "being erroneous" implies "being an opinion." Therefore "being an opinion" is a derivative philosophical character. And if further analysis reveals that an opinion is, let us say, a proposition plus some degree of inclination to believe or to disbelieve it, then "being a proposition," "being disbelief," etc., would thereby be revealed as derivative philosophical characters. Accordingly, the judgment expressed by the statement, "That these words are printed in blue ink is an opinion," would be a derivative particular philosophical fact; whereas the judgment expressed by the statement, "That these words are printed in blue ink is erroneous," would be a primitive particular philosophical fact.[2]

These are the sorts of particular facts with which philosophical theories are concerned, and by reference to which they are tested. These facts are different from the particular facts relevant to the theories of natural science, but they are facts equally, and experiental facts; and the testing of philo-

---

[2] What is a philosophical fact in each case is the judgment mentioned, i.e., the fact is that somebody makes these judgments. What the person who makes them asserts, however, may or may not also be a fact, i.e., be true.

The judgment expressed by the statement, "That these words are printed in blue ink is erroneous," may be otherwise expressed: "No, these words are not printed in blue ink." That is, it essentially consists in disagreement with the opinion that the words are printed in blue ink. For disagreement or agreement with an opinion one understands, no training is needed. It is a primitive capacity. Even the savage and the young child have it, although, of course, the opinions they are able to understand are relatively few. On the other hand, the judgment expressed by the statement, "That these words are printed in blue ink is an opinion" is a judgment which only a highly sophisticated person is capable of making; for it is not an act of agreement but an act of classification, for which the concept of "opinion," is indispensable. And this concept (which is more abstract than the relatively familiar one of "mere opinion," i.e., belief as contrasted with knowledge) is possessed only by persons epistemologically sensitized enough to discriminate at least in practice between opinion in general and either erroneous or sound opinion, and also between sound opinion and knowledge. This sensitiveness is derived (either at first hand, or more often at second hand) from reflection upon given cases of the application of such value-predicates as "erroneous," "sound," "known," etc.

sophical theories by reference to them is therefore as genuinely empirical testing. A philosophical theory, to the effect,
for instance, that, as suggested above, an opinion is a proposition plus one or another degree of inclination to believe or to
disbelieve it, must, in order to be acceptable, fit among others
the particular philosophical fact expressed by the statement,
"That these words are printed in blue ink is an opinion,"
and also the particular philosophical fact expressed by the
statement, " 'Are these words printed in blue ink?' is not an
opinion."

2. *The Empirical Generalizations of Philosophy.*—By empirical
generalization of the primitive philosophical facts, empirical
norms—empirical axiological laws—are obtained. They are
the philosophical analogues of the empirical laws which, in
the field of natural science, describe the commonly recognized
(nontechnical) properties of various kinds of things—for
instance, the property or law of steel, that it rusts in moist
air;[3] the property or law of wax, that it is fusible by heat,
etc. An example of a philosophical law obtained by the
empirical generalizing of derivative instead of primitive
particular facts would be the one expressed by the statement,
"All entities expressible by sentences of the form 'S is P' or
'S is not P' are opinions."

3. *Primitive Philosophical Facts, and Therefore Also Empirical
Norms, Always "Functions" of Specific Persons.*—All facts
primitive for philosophy are appraisals, and an appraisal
essentially involves three things: something appraised, some
appraiser of it, and the sort of appraisal made. Therefore, no
statement of an appraisal is complete unless it specifies all
three of these constituents. That is, every statement of an

---

[3] This illustration is borrowed from Campbell's *What Is Science?*, p. 40.

appraisal, and therefore every statement of a philosophical primitive and likewise of a norm, whether empirical or not, must, in order to be unambiguous, have the form "the appraisal made of entity (or entities) E by person (or persons) P is of kind A." Accordingly, a peculiarity of primitive philosophical facts (and of value-facts in general) is that such facts are all essentially relative to a given person or group, in the sense that some particular person or group—and, moreover, an appraising one—is an intrinsic constituent of all of them. Specification of the person or group concerned may, as we have seen, be made either denotatively, or else descriptively, in terms of its "position," i.e., of its relation, to the entity appraised.

The primitive facts of natural science, on the other hand, are not in this sense essentially relative to—are not "functions" of—some person. They are indeed likewise objects of judgment by persons, but in them the object of judgment does not itself contain a person as one of its intrinsic constituents. Accordingly, whereas mention of a person or persons is indispensable to the adequate description of a primitive philosophical fact or of an axiological law, mention of a person in the description of a primitive fact (or law) of natural science is irrelevant in all cases except those where the fact happens to be specifically an anthropological one; and in these "person" means only a human body making perceptually public responses to perceptually public stimuli.

4. *The Task, the Nature, and the Validity of Philosophical Theories.*—The sort of situation which calls for construction of a philosophical theory is this: A given philosophical predicate is spontaneously applied by given persons to a variety of entities which, so far as observation directly reveals, seem to have in common no character invariably lack-

ing in the variety of other entities to which the opposite of that predicate is also spontaneously applied by these persons. The task of theory is to explain this situation conceptually, and this is done by constructing conceptually the unperceived character satisfying that requirement. This character is *ex hypothesi* a hidden one, since otherwise merely abstractive observation would be capable of exhibiting it, and theory construction, i.e., invention of it, would not be needed. That, in spite of its hiddenness, its presence or absence in a given entity is nevertheless empirically ascertainable is due to the fact that its presence or absence is not ascertained by direct observation, but only through the indirect test specified in the "method" which, as we have seen, always has to accompany the "definition" proposed by the theory for the given predicate.

The validity of the theory—the "reality" of the character it invents—is a matter, first, of whether it fits the facts which actually gave rise to the need for a theory, and, second, of whether it successfully predicts facts other than the ones it was specifically intended to fit. More specifically, the two tests are as follows:

The facts which actually gave rise to the need for a theory consisted in the spontaneous application by given persons of the given predicate and its opposite, respectively, to two sets of given entities; and the first test is whether applicability of the predicate and its opposite respectively to these two sets of entities is deducible from the theory.

The second test is whether some other sorts of entities, which were not taken into consideration in the devising of the theory but to which (according to the theory) the given predicate, or its opposite, should be applicable, turn out to be entities to which respectively the given predicate or its opposite are in fact spontaneously applied by the same persons.

A theory which satisfies the first test, and for the validity of which there is also considerable evidence of the kind defined by the second test, provides a basis for rational settlement of cases of doubt or conflict among the applications of the given predicate or of its opposite by the given persons; for to settle such cases rationally consists in deciding them in a manner whose theory is identical with a theory already acknowledged by these persons as adequate to explain the majority or the most confident of their own applications of that predicate and its opposite. A theory whose validity has been confirmed in this manner moreover makes possible the discovery—deductively from it—of new (i.e., nonspontaneous) applications (affirmative or negative) of the given predicate which are valid, in the sense of coherent in principle with those already made by the persons concerned.

Before passing to concrete illustrations of the manner in which the empirical tests of validity of philosophical theories are applied in practice, we must reply briefly to an objection which might suggest itself at this point.

5. *Two Ways of "Knowing" the Meaning of a Philosophical Predicate.*—As already pointed out, a philosophical theory reduces in essentials to a definition of a philosophical predicate, together with a method for the empirical identification of cases of the *definiens*. But the definition cannot be an arbitrary one, since there are tests it must meet. A question therefore suggests itself as to how it can be needed at all. For either one knows what a term means or one does not and, since most philosophical predicates are terms in common use, one must already know what they mean. Otherwise one would not be able to use them.

The answer obviously is that there are ways and ways of "knowing what a term means." More particularly, there are two. One of them may be described as intuitive, superficial, and good only for everyday practical purposes. To "know the meaning" of a word, in this sense, consists in being able to act appropriately in response to familiar sentences in which the word is used, and in being able to use the word in sentences ourselves. This is the way in which every English-speaking person knows, for instance, what is meant by the word "time": he is able to act appropriately in response to such sentences as, "You have time for lunch before the train starts"; "What time is it?"; "How did you spend your time?" But only very few persons have, in addition to this, also the analytical and discursive knowledge of the meaning of "time" needed for theoretical purposes—the sort of knowledge of its meaning, namely, that would enable them to answer adequately the question "What is time?" or questions that presuppose knowledge of the answer to it. The knowledge which philosophical theory seeks of the meaning of the predicates with which it is concerned is knowledge of this second kind. If we distinguish between (1) a term T, (2) that which it means, M, i.e., the meant, and (3) the conceptual analysis of M, we may say that when M is a philosophical character (and T therefore a philosophical predicate), conceptual analysis of M (as distinguished from directly observational analysis of it) is what philosophical theorizing undertakes.

6. *Two Kinds of "Meaning" of a Term.*—Terms, and among them those whose meaning philosophy investigates, obviously do not have a meaning in themselves but only as used by a given person or persons. When, however, we speak of the use made of a given predicate, we may be referring either to the applications made of it—i.e., to the variety of subjects of which we predicate it—or to the implications of it, i.e., to

the set of attributes we assert of anything by means of the given predicate. In the first case, "to mean" is essentially to orient us to—to call our attention to, to indicate to us—certain things (as to the attributes of which we may know very little); whereas in the second case "to mean" is essentially to prepare us *for* or prepare us *to*—to prepare us for some experience, or prepare us to act in some particular way. The first may be called the indicative or monstrative use of a term, and the second its quiddative use. The distinction is ultimately that between *where* and *what*, between the place of something and the properties of it. It is of first importance for the theory of knowledge and should not be blurred by, for instance, using the word "referent" indiscriminately for both. The distinction is customarily described as one between the denotation and the connotation, or the extension and the intension of a term. These two pairs of terms often are used synonymously, although both pairs, I believe, are needed to mark a further important distinction. This matter, however, which it seems to me even the best writers have not satisfactorily discussed, would demand a chapter in itself and need not be further pursued for our present purpose. I need say only that I shall use the terms "extension" or "extensional meaning" and "intension" or "intensional meaning," or the terms "application" and "implication," as J. N. Keynes does—to refer to the general distinction made irrespective of further refinements.

The matter is brought up here only because the application and the implication of a term are indissolubly connected and because of the bearings of this fact upon the method of empirical investigation of the meaning of given terms. Although the fact of cardinal importance here is familiar enough, its methodological bearings are only too often ignored. That fact is that the moment either the application or the implication of a term is given, the other is thereby implicitly determined, and therefore cannot be independently given but must be (or must have been) discovered empirically. Conversely, there is no possibility of empirical inquiry into either the application or the implication of a term, unless the other is given to begin with. That is, as cannot be repeated too often, there is no such thing as a genuine problem without data; and in particular there is no genuine problem as to the implication of a term except as relative to given applications of it.

The indissoluble connection between application and implication is evident enough if we turn to examples. If, for instance, it is given that the term "tree" is applied to this, that, and that object, then it cannot also be given that that term implies certain characters, such as having feathers, etc., which any of these objects happens not to possess. For the term "tree" can then imply none but characters possessed by all of them; and which characters these are can ultimately be decided only by observation of these objects. What we can stipulate in such a case is only that the term shall be used to imply only certain ones of these characters, e.g., those which together differentiate the objects to which "tree" is applied from any objects that resemble these in some stated respect but to which the name tree is in fact denied.

On the other hand, if it is given to begin with that the term tree implies possession at least of a certain character C, then it cannot be also given that it applies to a certain object, for this object may happen not to possess it. The term can be applied to—predicated of—none but objects that have character C, and only empirical investigation, not stipulation, can tell us which ones have it. What we can stipulate, however, is that the term shall be applied only to certain ones of these objects, e.g., only to such of them as have in addition certain other characters.

In practice, when we are called upon to investigate the meaning of a term in common use, we do not start with a *tabula rasa*, on which arbitrary stipulation would have to write the data of the problem. Rather, we already know (whether intuitively or discursively) some characters which the term implies and some entities to which it applies—all these characters being *in fact* possessed by all these entities. Our problem is then either that of discovering which other entities also possess all of these characters (the latter then functioning as data of our problem), or that of discovering what other characters are all possessed by all the given entities (the latter then functioning as data of our problem).

In the light of these remarks and of the considerations summarized in the preceding sections of this chapter, we shall now attempt to state in the form of a number of precepts the sort of method which can yield genuine knowledge in theoretical philosophy.

7. *Precepts of the Method of Knowledge in Theoretical Philosophy.*—Let us recall to begin with the illustration from the field of ethics previously employed, namely, the problem of the nature of right and wrong. To be even theoretically—to say nothing of practically—soluble the problem to which these words only allude must be stated in a manner specifying its data, for, once more, a problem without data is a question about nothing. As that problem presents itself on a given occasion, an adequate statement of it might be as follows: What theory of wrongness and rightness explains conceptually the application of the predicate "wrong" to, for instance, killing, stealing, and adultery, and of the predicate "right" to, for instance, kindness, honesty, and veracity, by persons P, Q, R? In so stating the problem, we are obeying the first of the methodological precepts that follow from all our

preceding discussion. This precept is: *Specify the data of the problem.*

There is nothing revolutionary about this precept, which only articulates the procedure ordinary common sense would dictate. Yet in philosophy it is only too often unheeded, the data of the problems attacked being assumed to be already understood, or being only alluded to or hinted at instead of explicitly stated. This first precept, moreover, loses some of its triteness if we particularize it specifically to fit problems such as the one here exemplified, where what we seek is the intensional meaning—the "implication"—of a given term; for it then becomes: *List the applications of the given term, and the applications of the contrary term from which we seek to distinguish it, that are to be explained.* To comply with this precept is to give such lists as: "killing is wrong"; "adultery is wrong"; "stealing is wrong"; "kindness is right"; "honesty is right"; "veracity is right."

When this is done, the second precept readily suggests itself, namely: *In the listed applications, substitute for the term the proposed definition of it. If this substitution leaves unchanged the truth-value of the respective applications, the proposed definition "fits" the term as applied to the entities mentioned in them.* That is, it explains these applications of the term in the sense that they can be deduced from the proposed definition of it.

It may be asked, however, how we can tell whether or not the truth-values remain unchanged—more specifically, how we can tell whether the truth-value of, for instance, "stealing is a case of D" (where D is the *definiens* of a proposed definition of "wrong"), is the same as the truth-value of "stealing is wrong." The answer is as follows: That the truth-value of the latter is "truth" is known to us to begin with *ex hypothesi*, for as emphasized earlier the statement "stealing is wrong" formulates simply the spontaneous disapproval of stealing

by the given persons P, Q, R. We assume here only that
when they assert their disapproval of stealing they are not
dissembling their actual attitude. As regards the truth-value
of "stealing is a case of D," we are enabled to ascertain
whether it is "truth" or "falsity" by the very "method for
identification of cases of the *definiens*" which as we have seen
must accompany a proposed definition whenever that definition is a theoretical one instead of one obtained directly by
abstractive analysis of observed facts.[4]

It may be asked further what precept can be given for discovery of a theoretical definition which, in the sense stated,
"fits" the specified applications. The answer is that no precept for this can be given other than: Try, and if you don't
succeed, try again and again. Thinking of a definition which
will fit is a matter of the fertility and sagacity of the investigator's mind. The method of trial and error, if it can be
described as a method at all rather than as absence of method,
is the only one available here; and we can give a precept only
for determining whether a definition we somehow came to
think of does or does not fit.

The second precept above formulates the method for
determining whether or not a definition proposed for a given
term fits the applications of that term which it was specifically devised to fit. As we have seen, however, a definition
is not authoritatively explanatory unless it has in addition

---

[4] A definition proposed for a term, no matter whether obtained by would-be
abstractive analysis of observations or by speculation, is not acceptable unless its
definiens can be substituted for the term in any statement whatever where the term
occurs, without thereby altering the truth-value of the proposition formulated by
the statement. The precept given in the text therefore applies, no matter how the
proposed definition has been obtained; but if it has been obtained by abstractive
analysis of observed facts, the question whether it fits or does not fit these facts
can be answered by more careful direct scrutiny of them. If, on the other hand, the
definition was obtained by invention, whether or not it fits can be ascertained only
through the indirect test specified in the "method" with which any speculative
definition has to be accompanied.

the capacity to predict successfully spontaneous applications of the term that were not considered at all in the devising of the definition; that is, spontaneous applications of it that were no part of the specific facts that gave rise to the problem and in terms of which it was formulated. The precept that governs the testing of a proposed definition in respect to that capacity is as follows: *Consider kinds of entities other than those figuring in the data of the problem and determine, by the method which accompanies the proposed definition, whether, according to that definition of the given term, the term is, or on the contrary is not, applicable to entities of these other kinds. If its applicability and inapplicability to such entities (according to the definition) coincides with the application and nonapplication spontaneously made of it to those very entities by the same persons P, Q, R, then the definition is thereby shown to possess to this extent the required sort of predictive capacity.*

These are the chief precepts by compliance with which the status of knowledge—probable knowledge—can be obtained for the definitions which theoretical philosophy is so largely occupied in seeking. The procedure these precepts dictate perhaps seems artificial and remote from anything ever actually occurring in philosophical investigations. But any appearance of artificiality is, I believe, only a case of the sort of result which formal description of the familiar almost always has. The formal description of the process of hitting a golf ball, for instance, which could be formulated through analysis of it by slow-motion pictures, would similarly seem artificial. Again, if a person, even one whom we have known all our lives, were minutely dissected and the relations of the pieces described, we should doubtless say that what we are offered is nothing much like him. What analysis exhibits is always more or less unfamiliar even when the analysis is correct, and this just because analysis does reveal within the familiar certain features that had not hitherto been individually discriminated. Moreover, examples are not lacking in which the procedure described by these precepts has been actually used by philosophers, even if less systematically than would be desirable or than would have been the case if their use of it, instead of being instinctive, had been fully conscious and deliberate. The last of the precepts given, for instance, is the very one Thomas Reid was following when, to demonstrate the invalidity of Hume's definition of the "cause" of a phenomenon as the antecedent which the phenomenon invariably has followed in our past experience, he pointed out that according to this definition the term "causation" would be applicable to the relation of day to night and of night to day, whereas in fact our spontaneous judgment refuses to apply that term to this relation.

It may be added that what is essential, in order that our method of philosophical investigation be knowledge-yielding, is in the first place that the nature of the data relevant to problems of definition of philosophical terms in general be clearly realized, and in the second that the data of the specific problem of definition to which we address ourselves at a given time be clearly present to mind. Formal listing of them is a device for making sure that they are present to mind, and are the same in the minds of all parties to the given investigation. If in a given case we are already sure of this, the formal listing of them would only be pedantic.

I shall now give illustrations, in terms of some familiar philosophical problems, of the procedure which the precepts stated would dictate.

8. *Illustrations of Procedure.*—Let us consider first the problem of the nature of reality. The first question which the precepts require us to ask is, "What are the data of the

problem?"; and the attempt to answer it immediately forces us to decide which one of two different but very similar-sounding questions is the one we seek to answer. They are "What being is real?" and "What is being real?" The second calls for an account of the character constituting the criterion of realness as distinguished from unrealness, whereas the first calls for mention of the kind or kinds of being which possess that character. The second is a question as to the intension of the adjective real, and if it is a question susceptible of a nonarbitrary answer, its datum can consist only of an extension spontaneously given to the adjective. The first on the contrary is a question as to the extension of that adjective, and a nonarbitrary answer to it can be reached only if we have as datum of the problem an intension spontaneously given to the adjective real.

Problems of philosophical theory are for the most part concerned with the intension which theoretical purposes demand for a given philosophical term; but occasionally a question arises as to extension instead. An example would be the controversy between Bradley and McTaggart as to whether the individual or only the whole universe is real. The intensional assumption they both took as datum might be stated in some such way as this: "To be real is to be susceptible of being taken without contradiction as ontologically ultimate." This, however, can hardly be claimed to state the intension spontaneously ascribed to the term real, even by them. It states much rather a theory they both accept as to the intension of the term, although I can hardly imagine what spontaneous extensional data it would fit. But even if that definition of "to be real" were wholly arbitrary, it would, under a certain proviso, enable those who do take it as datum to settle a controversy among them as to whether individuals, or the universe as a whole, or both, or neither, or mind, or matter, etc., are real. The proviso is that that definition of real should be accompanied by the stipulation of a method for deciding whether any given thing is or is not "susceptible of being taken without contradiction as ontologically ultimate." I do not believe that this proviso was met even informally, and if it was not, the controversy, because pervaded by ambiguity, remains insoluble irrespective of whether the definition of "to be real" used in it as datum is or is not arbitrary.

The problem of "the nature of reality" has in most cases been discussed without preliminary discrimination between the two questions "What being is real?" and "What is being real?"; without realization that both these questions cannot be raised at once, since each requires as datum what in the other is the quaesitum; without realization that the only nonarbitrary data for either consist of uses spontaneously made of the adjective real; and without initial statement of such data. It is therefore little wonder that no authoritative answer has yet been found to the question as to "the nature of reality." If, however, we ask, "What definition of real would explain our spontaneous assertion that Spain is a real country but Utopia is not?" we have a genuine problem, which is susceptible of solution because we are furnished with its data, viz., with an extension of "real" which any intension proposed for this adjective must fit. It may be said, perhaps, that although this is a genuine and soluble problem, it is not the one ontologists have been attempting to answer. This may well be true, for "real" possibly has other kinds of use than that made of it in the statement that Spain is a real country. I insist only that if the ontologists' problem is to be a genuine and soluble one, its data have to be specified to begin with, and that, if they are not to be arbitrary, they can consist only of common spontaneous predications of the adjective real—if not about Spain, then about some explicitly mentioned other sort of entity. If the ontologist is unable to mention them, then neither we nor he himself know what his problem is.

As another example, we may take the question "What is it to exist?" which, although it is often regarded as synonymous with "What is it to be real?" is as I believe nevertheless distinct from it. Suppose that instead of asking "What is it to exist?" we ask "What definition of 'to exist' would explain our spontaneous assertions that, for instance, black swans exist but green swans do not, and that a square root of 9 exists but a square root of 3 does not?" We have then mentioned the data of the problem—the facts which any proposed definition of "to exist" is to fit—and we are therefore in position to ascertain empirically, in accordance with the second and third precepts above, whether a given definition of it does or does not fit the facts.[5]

Again, the problem of the relation between mind and nature presupposes an answer to the questions "What is mind?" and "What is nature?" So long as they are phrased in this way, the correctness or incorrectness of any answer proposed to them remains impossible to check. But we may rephrase them, asking, "What definitions of 'mental' and of 'physical' would account for the spontaneous common assertions that wondering, remembering, imagining, are mental events, whereas breathing, walking, eating, are physical events?" Then, because we have in this way been furnished with the facts which the definitions sought are desired to fit, it becomes possible for us to show whether any proposed definitions do or do not fit them.

---

[5] In a paper entitled "On Our Knowledge of Existents," I have offered a definition of "to exist" which seems to me to fit these facts. See *Proceedings, 7th International Congress of Philosophy*, pp. 163–7.

These illustrations will make clear how a realization of
the nature of the data of the philosophical problems we
raise, and an explicit statement of these data at the outset,
open the way to genuinely knowledge-yielding procedure—
as described in the precepts given—in the field of philosophical inquiry. The knowledge obtained in this manner will,
like scientific knowledge in other fields, be for the most part
probable knowledge only. That is, what we shall know will
usually be only that a certain philosophical assertion is, on
specified evidence we have at the time, more probably true
than a certain other. This knowledge, although at first
fragmentary and not organized into a system, will, because
it is based on facts of philosophical experience, have the
verifiability and the capacity for genuine growth which has
been so conspicuously lacking in philosophy as compared
with the other sciences, and which a philosophical system
constructed a priori cannot possess, however formally perfect
it may be.

The systematic organizing of philosophical knowledge—
the ascertaining of the mutual relations of the philosophical
facts already discovered at a given time, and the looking
specifically for the other facts needed to fill gaps still existing
—is a proper and necessary task in the field of philosophy as
in any other. Its method is the same in philosophy as in any
other field, and it can be begun as soon as any knowledge, as
material to be organized, has been won. The great obstacles
to real progress in philosophy have been, it seems to me, the
lack of clear ideas as to the subject matter distinctive of
philosophy, as to the general nature and function of theory
construction, as to the sort of data by reference to which the
validity of philosophical theories can be empirically tested,
and as to the method by which this testing must proceed. It
is on these obscure matters that I have specifically attempted

to shed such light as I believe I see. I have therefore said little or nothing as to the criticism of theories, philosophical or other, in respect to their internal consistency or formal rigor. This is a matter commonly much better understood, and I have therefore concentrated instead on the problem of method for criticism of philosophical theories in respect to their fitting or failing to fit the facts they concern, and on the problem of the general nature of these facts.

9. *Philosophy, Nature, Mind and Language.*—In earlier chapters, the philosophical sciences were distinguished from the natural, the mental, and the formal sciences on the basis of the subject matter peculiar to each. The subject matter distinctive of philosophy, it was contended, is appraisals—spontaneous particular appraisals—and whatever turns out to be implicit in them. That of the natural sciences consists of facts perceptually public and whatever proves to be implicit in them. That of the mental sciences is facts introspectively ascertainable plus whatever they imply. And the subject matter of the formal sciences consists of facts created by stipulations as to relations of words or other discursive entities to one another, plus such other facts as are implicit in these stipulations.

The question might still be asked, however, how these four sorts of subject matter are related to one another. Do some of them perhaps in part overlap? Or are one or more of them perhaps species of the rest? Or are they wholly independent? More specifically, is mind perhaps only a part of nature? Are pure logic and mathematics parts of the science of mind, or perhaps of the science of nature? And are appraisals facts of mind or facts of nature? Little or no attention has been given to these questions in the present discussion, and the effort has been made not to base anything said concerning philosophy and its method upon any assumed particular answer to them. Accordingly, if the account that has been given of philosophy as normative science or science of appraisals holds at all, it holds no matter what may be the right answers to these questions. This, of course, is as it should be, since our inquiry belongs to the field of philosophical metatheory rather than directly to that of philosophical theory. Because of this, any discussion of these important and interesting questions is best left to some future occasion.

Index

Index

241

O

Observation, 157–61, 171
Opposition and distinction, 44–5
Organism and Environment, 206
Otto, M. C., 5, 49–50
Our Knowledge of the External World, 63

P

Philosophy
  and faith, 13–30
  generality of, 3–11, 64–6
  of life, 49–50
  and literature about the cosmos, 31–48
  and logic, 63–72, 82–5
  and logical syntax, 87–109
  method of, 13–4, 72, 114–5, 211–5
    illustrated in ethics, 174–92
    illustrated in epistemology, 192–5
    illustrated in problem of reality,
      232–5
  precepts of, 228–32
  according to
    Collingwood, 35–6
    Dewey, 52–3
    Hoernlé, 19–21
    Langer, 74–5
    Russell, 67–9
    Urban, 26–30
  and natural science, xvii–xx, 3–11,
    33–5, 75–82
  and religion, 9, 22–3
  and social problems, 49–62
  and study of meanings, 73–86
  subject matter of, 137–55, 116, 218–22,
    237
  seeks knowledge, 113–6
  traditional, 31–3, 66–7
  value of, 45–6, 54, 66–7
  and wisdom, 197–9, 210–5
Philosophy and Logical Syntax, 87 (*see also*
  Carnap, R.)
Philosophical Method, 31–48
Physics, the Elements, 126
Play, 207–8
Practice of Philosophy, The, 9–10 (*see also*
  Langer, S. K.)
Pragmatism, 50–62, 214–5
Principia Mathematica, 63
Property, 157–8

Propositions
  metaphysical, 87–9
  pseudo-, 88
  Russell's view of, 65–6
Psychology
  gestalt, 134–6
  introspective, 129–34
Purpose, 203–7
Pythagoras, 159

R

Rashevsky, N., 4
Reality, problem of, 148–9, 232–5
Reason, 157–61, 171
Reason and Nature, 78, 127
Reconstruction in Philosophy, 50
Reid, Thomas, 232
Relativity, in ethics, 187–8
Religion, 9, 22–3
Rueff, J., 176–7, 181
Russell, B., 24, 63–72, 76, 83

S

Santayana, G., 58
Schlick, Moritz, xvii, 3
Schopenhauer, A., 56–7
Science
  definition of a, 115–6
  formal, 116, 127–9, 237
  language of, 89
  mental, 117, 129–34, 237
  method of, 217–8
  natural, 116–8, 125–7, 160, 237
  and philosophy (*see* Philosophy, and
    natural science)
  physical, 76–7, 85
  rational, 73–4, 77–85
  social, 117
  subject matter of, 70
Scientific Thought, 81
Sentences
  pseudo-object, 92–5, 97–8
  real-object, 92–3, 97–8
  syntactical, 89, 92, 95
  translatability of, 93–107
Skepticism, 26–8
Socrates, 73
Some Problems of Philosophy, 10

Species
  co-ordinate, 37–9
  "degrees" of, 43–4
  "overlapping" of, 33–9
Spencer, H., 5–8
Spinoza, B., 84–5
Stevens, S. S., 126
Studies in Contemporary Metaphysics (*see* Hoernlé, R. F. A.)
Synonymy and truth value, 96–7, 105–6
Syntax, logical, 87–109
Subject matter
  how defined, 113–23
  of formal science, 127–9, 237
  of mental science, 129–34, 237
  of natural science, 125–7, 237
  of philosophy, 137–55, 218–22, 237

T

Technical terms
  Collingwood's view of, 35–6, 46
  nature and value of, 47–8
Technique of Theory Construction, The, 168
Telism, 203–8
Textbook of Psychology, A, 131
Theory, 158–9
  vs. conjecture, 161–2
  as explanatory conjecture, 162–7
  ethical, 174–92
  nature of philosophical, 173–95

  task of philosophical, 222–3, 224–5
  test of, 168–9
  validity of philosophical, 223–4
Thinking
  free and servile, 60–2
  and knowing, 54–5
  and logic, 107–9
  nature and value of, 56–9
Thompson, D' Arcy W., 4
Titchener, E. B., 130–4
"Transcendental Aesthetic," 68–9
Translation, 93–107

U

Unity, search for, 14–9
Unity of Science, The, 88
Urban, W. M., 23–30

V

Valuation (*see* Appraisal)
Verification, 87–8, 168–9

W

Wisdom, viii–ix, 113–4, 197–9, 208–15
Whewell, W., 47, 168, 171, 219
Whitehead, A. N., 63, 76
Woodger, J. H., 168